D1119227

The **Parrot** companion

Low, Rosemary.
The parrot companion :
caring for parrots, maca
2006.
33305211821883
la   02/05/07

the
Parrot
companion

Caring for Parrots, Macaws, Budgies, Cockatiels & More

Rosemary Low

FIREFLY BOOKS

A FIREFLY BOOK

Published by Firefly Books Ltd. 2006

Copyright © 2006 New Holland Publishers (UK) Ltd
Text Copyright © 2006 Rosemary Low
Illustration Copyright © 2006 Louwra Marais
Photo Copyright © 2006 Rosemary Low, except as noted on page 192

All rights reserved. No part of this publication may be reproduced, stored in a retrieval
system, or transmitted in any form or by any means, electronic, mechanical, photocopying,
recording or otherwise, without the prior written permission of the Publisher.

First printing

**Publisher Cataloging-in-Publication Data
(U.S.)**

Low, Rosemary.
   The parrot companion : caring for parrots,
macaws, budgies, cockatiels & more / Rosemary Low.
[193] p. : col. photos. ;   cm.
Includes index.
Summary: Guide to caring for 25 of the most
common breeds of parrots with a focus on choosing
the right bird and keeping it healthy, including tips
on training, equipment, nutrition, grooming, and
principal characteristics of each breed.
ISBN-13: 978-1-55407-199-9 (pbk.)
ISBN-10: 1-55407-199-2 (pbk.)
1. Parrots. I. Title.
636.6/865 dc22   SF473.P3.L69 2006

Published in the United States by
Firefly Books (U.S.) Inc.
P.O. Box 1338, Ellicott Station
Buffalo, New York 14205

Printed in Singapore

**Library and Archives Canada Cataloguing
in Publication**

Low, Rosemary
   The parrot companion : caring for parrots,
macaws, budgies, cockatiels & more / Rosemary Low.
Includes index.
ISBN-13: 978-1-55407-199-9
ISBN-10: 1-55407-199-2
   1. Parrots. I. Title.
SF473.P3L683 2006   636.6'865   C2006-
901045-5

Published in Canada by
Firefly Books Ltd.
66 Leek Crescent
Richmond Hill, Ontario L4B 1H1

Contents

Parrots as pets

Parrot ownership is a much greater responsibility than most new parrot owners realize. The level of commitment necessary to prevent a parrot from developing behavioral problems is extremely high. Many potential owners tend to regard a parrot as a beautiful or amusing object, not as an individual that is almost as complex emotionally as a human. It is a highly social creature whose need for a close relationship, either with a human or with a member of its own kind, is central to its existence. When it is happy it can be the most wonderful companion known to humankind, but when denied this relationship its life will be sad and stressful and it could become unwanted and impossible to rehome.

Opposite: *A parrot is an emotionally complex creature whose needs must be understood.*

The decision to take on a parrot must therefore be thought through with great care. A number of factors should be considered with honesty.

Before buying a parrot you should ask yourself these questions:

- Are you an experienced animal/bird owner? Parrots are the most complicated and difficult birds to look after in the home. Experience with easier birds or animals is essential before taking on the most difficult.
- Can you commit yourself to caring for a parrot (or other psittacine bird) for 30 to 60 years? Finding a new home for a parrot is difficult and change of ownership causes stress to the bird.
- Can you dedicate one hour of one-to-one time with your parrot each day? Spending quality time with your bird is the best way to ensure a strong bond.
- Will you or other family members be in the house for at least 19 hours daily? A parrot

Below: *Owners need to spend a lot of time with their parrots.*

Opposite: *If you have asthma, the feather dust that parrots emit could worsen the condition.*

should not be left alone for more than five hours daily during the day. (A young bird will need 11 hours sleep at night and it will doze for two or three hours more during the day. An adult parrot needs at least nine hours sleep at night and it will doze during the afternoon.)

- Will you research the essential components of your parrot's diet so that it will not die prematurely of a dietary deficiency?

- Can you tolerate some damage in the house?

- Will you be able to stand the noise—especially when you are watching your favorite television program or attempting to have a telephone conversation?

If you answer "no" to any of these questions, think again. If all your answers are "yes," you could be a suitable person to look after a parrot, but you now need to consider two more ques-tions. If you smoke, can you give up smoking or never smoke in the vicinity of your parrot? If not, secondary smoke could kill your parrot after three or four years.

Do you have asthma or another respiratory problem? If so, the feather dust that parrots emit could exacerbate the condition and may harm your health. In the home, ventilators (or good ventilation) and ionizers are important aids to a healthy atmosphere. These pieces of equipment will minimize the dust that accumulates in the air from a parrot's plumage. Manufacturers state that ionizers can even attract virus particles out of the atmosphere. There is no doubt that they remove dust. For this reason, you should frequently wipe the area around an ionizer with a damp cloth. Seek professional advice on the correct size of ionizers and ventilators for the room in question.

This is very important for anyone who suffers from asthma. Nevertheless, the most effective way of eliminating dust is to spray and bathe your parrots frequently (especially Grays and cockatoos).

The reason why many people find that a parrot tries their patience beyond endurance is the noise. Also consider that some parrots are too clever at mimicry. Could you live with a parrot that emits the sound of a car alarm a dozen times a day, or the cuckoo clock, the birds in the garden, or the microwave timer? It might copy the telephone so realistically that you would not be able to distinguish its mimicry from the real thing.

Nevertheless, living with a parrot can be a great source of satisfaction and entertainment. For people who live alone, or for the housebound, a tame and affectionate parrot can give them a reason to get up every morning and face the day with pleasure. Depending on the species, parrots can be playful, humorous, loquacious, mischievous, and affectionate. They can even prevent troubled people from becoming self-occupied and depressed. This might sound like an exaggeration, but they can even save lives. Just like dogs, parrots have been known to warn their owners of fires at night or of the presence of intruders.

If you treat parrots with tender affection, they will return this with interest. If you shout at them or become aggressive, they will mimic this behavior. A parrot is like a child: it is, to a degree, the reflection of the adults who raised it. However, like a human, it has the capacity to show strong feelings toward individuals—love or intense

Opposite: When macaws are kept in the home, their loud calls can severely test the patience of many people.

Below: A parrot needs to live with someone who truly enjoys its company.

dislike. When the latter emotion is directed toward a family member who brought it up or who is most interested in it, the result is usually disappointment and, if no one else is interested in the bird, possibly neglect—or even abuse. In such circumstances strongly encourage another member of the family to take an interest in the parrot as his or her special friend. However, you cannot force this interest where it does not exist. In some cases it might be better to find a new home for the parrot with someone it really likes.

It is important to know that parrots, unlike dogs, do not like someone just because he or she gives them attention and food. The parrot might dislike the owner for a reason that is not clear. It could be that they dislike the person's voice. On the other hand, parrots are extremely sensitive and observant birds. They pick up emotions, including fear. Someone who is afraid of a parrot seldom gets along with it and the parrot soon dominates that person, using biting to get its way.

Parrots prefer people who are quiet and calm. Those who shout, wave their arms around, and behave unpredictably are unlikely to be their chosen companions. Most parrots do not like children because their movements are so fast and erratic. However, some parrots, notably Amazons, like children with shrill voices because this stimulates them to be noisy.

Parrots enjoy being in a busy household with much activity that they can observe, and with people who interact with them, or being in a home with one or two people who can devote a lot of time to them. The worst scenario is where they are treated as little more than ornaments, given no freedom outside the cage and no affection. This is a living death for a sociable and intelligent creature like a parrot.

These days most parrots that are bought as companions have been hand-reared from the age of a few days or a few weeks for this very purpose. They have not been socialized with other parrots, but isolated in a household as soon as they can feed themselves. Most of them identify with humans more than with other parrots. This makes them extremely demanding companions. They crave and need frequent human attention. If they do not receive it, they develop serious behavioral problems (see Chapter 5). This is why it is vitally important to be aware of the level of commitment and amount of time needed to prevent this common outcome of buying a parrot.

Above: *A cockatoo becomes excessively noisy at home if it does not receive sufficient attention.*
Opposite: Aratinga *conures, such as the* Golden-capped, Jendaya, *and* Sun, *have loud voices and are more suitable as aviary birds.*

Young, hand-reared parrots are extremely appealing, and some species, especially cockatoos, are very cuddly and affectionate. This leads to impulse buying. When the novelty of owning a young parrot has worn off, neglect sets in and the parrot's behavior—screaming, seed-flinging, or feather plucking—means that it is no longer a welcome member of the family. No one should ever buy a parrot with the thought that if they don't like it they can sell it or give it away. Sadly, there are so many unwanted parrots that this can prove difficult. Equally important is that changing homes is emotionally disturbing, especially for a young parrot. It results in insecurity, and this again leads to behavioral problems. If you buy a parrot you will influence its psychological well-being for the rest of its life, even if it does not remain with you.

Note the wise words of one man who worked in two different bird "sanctuaries," collecting unwanted parrots from owners. He wrote: "Most people only see parrots at zoos or animal parks. They are well-behaved, properly looked after, and usually very endearing and amusing, talking and doing tricks. They seem like ideal pets, those that will give many hours of amusement and always be a conversation topic when guests arrive. What owners often do not realize is that for every hour of amusement there is at least two hours of hard work, cleaning, feeding, and training. The cost of food, toys, and a properly sized cage can be very expensive. In the expanse of a zoo the squawks of a macaw or cockatoo do not seem too loud, but a macaw squawking in your living room is deafening and can become a problem, especially with the neighbours."

Parrots have long memories; indeed, I believe that large parrots have memories that are equal to those of humans. Consider that many wild-caught parrots, especially Grays, are forever terrified of human hands and this can only be because they never forget the cruel and rough treatment they received on being captured.

To overcome the bird's fear requires an enormous amount of patience from the human caregiver. Patience is a vital requirement of the parrotkeeper, and he or she must be naturally sympathetic toward animals. This is not such a common quality as one might imagine, and it seems to be inherent rather than acquired. To be a caring parrot owner you need to be able to try to work out how your parrot sees the world and what it needs and likes. You also need to learn to "read" its behavior. This is based on careful observation and thought.

Sensitive, thoughtful, caring people who spend a lot of time at home usually make the best owners. Their parrots are unlikely to be unduly noisy because their owners fulfill their needs. A problem can arise, however, when such a person acquires a second parrot, or a third, or a fourth. Jealousy is an emotion well known to parrots, the outcome of which can be very unpleasant: they have been known to attack their owners or other parrots (see Chapter 4).

The prospective purchaser should also be aware that many parrots, usually males, can become very aggressive during the breeding season and will attack family members. This is another reason why parrots are often unsuitable for families with small children. Many parrots have injured adults seriously at such times, so children are even more vulnerable. Also, while a devoted individual can tolerate these periods, knowing that they will pass, all too often in a family situation the verdict on the parrot is: "Get rid of it!" Unfortunately, a parrot can cause a large amount of disharmony in a family. Many parrot owners have heard the ultimatum: "Either that bird goes or I do."

It should also be realized that parrots and other pets might not get along. Or they might become best friends! Parrots acquired after some dog breeds are resident in the house, especially gun dogs, are at risk from the dog's natural instinct to kill or fetch.

Need I say too that parrots are not for the house-proud? Unless their wings are clipped, most parrots will cause damage to furniture, drapes, or other expensive items at some stage. This is not the parrot's fault. The blame lies with the owner for allowing unsupervised access and for failing to provide a dedicated area, such as a play stand.

A parrot is a naturally destructive bird with a need to gnaw continually, so another fact that must be considered before deciding to purchase is the availability of branches of apple, willow, or hawthorn to keep it occupied.

Opposite: *Two parrots might become best friends, such as these young Yellow-naped Amazons.*
Left: *This Blue and Yellow Macaw thrives on love and a close relationship with its owner.*

2

Which species is right for you?

There are approximately 250 species of parrots, so choosing one as a companion may be bewildering at first. However, only about 180 species are well known or fairly well known in captivity, and the number commonly kept as pets is very much less than that. In different countries, availability and popularity of species also dictate what you can buy. The universal favorites include Gray Parrots, Amazons, caiques, conures, Cockatiels, and Budgerigars. This chapter contains information that will help you to determine which parrot species is best suited to your needs.

Opposite: *Lorikeets are among the more difficult parrots to care for as companions.*

The factors influencing the potential human companionship of an individual bird depend on:

- the degree to which it has been socialized with people;
- the amount of time the owner spends with it and his or her ability to constantly and consistently treat it with love, sympathy, and patience;
- the owner's attitude to kind, but firm, discipline and training;
- the personality of the bird. Some are happier in an aviary with their own species than interacting with humans. Unfortunately, this is not readily apparent in most young birds.

In choosing the species, personal preference and circumstances will play a large part, but certain practical aspects must be considered carefully. The development of various traits in a species depends mainly on how much attention it receives.

All parrots are noisy sometimes, but frequent screaming sessions usually indicate that the bird is frustrated, lonely, or bored. Important information for a prospective purchaser is the level of noise and the type of vocalizations of which a species is capable. How often a parrot yells is a different matter and is dependent on how well its needs, practical and psychological, are met.

To evaluate how noisy a species is, I have assessed the volume of its calls

(4 being the loudest) and their shrillness (*see* opposite). For example, a Cockatiel is not loud in comparison with a cockatoo, but the shrillness of its calls might be just as annoying as much louder calls. The ability to mimic is also assessed.

The voices of parrots

SPECIES	LOUDNESS	SHRILLNESS	TOTAL	MIMICRY
Amazon	3	0	3	2–3*
Budgerigar	1	0	1	2
Caique	2	1	3	1
Cockatiel	1	1	2	2
Cockatoo (white)	4	0	4	1
Conures, *Aratinga*	2–3	0	2–3	1–2
Conures, *Pyrrhura*	2	0	2	0–1
Eclectus Parrot	2–3	0	2–3	2
Gray Parrot	2	1	3	3
Lorikeet, Green-naped and Swainson's/Rainbow	1	1	2	1–2
Lovebird	1	0–1*	1–2	1
Macaw (large)	4	0	4	1
Parrotlet	1	0	1	1
Senegal Parrot and other small *Poicephalus*	2	1	3	2

* Dependent on species

Opposite: *The shrillness of a Cockatiel's call can be very annoying.*

If you have never kept a parrot before, it is wise to start with one of the smaller species, such as caiques and conures. Many first-time parrot buyers start too ambitiously with birds that they literally cannot handle. The new owner does not allow the parrot out of the cage because he or she is frightened of its potential to injure someone with its powerful beak. This is unfair, and condemns the parrot to a poor quality of life.

Small parrots, on the other hand, are usually approached with much more confidence. They embrace varied groups that have little in common apart from their size. Compared with larger species, small parrots have a number of advantages. They do not need large and high-priced accommodation and they are relatively inexpensive to feed. Most are readily available at a low or reasonable price; this indicates that, generally speaking, they are easy to breed. A number are extremely beautiful and several are available in a range of color mutations. In short, they can be the ideal introduction to parrotkeeping.

Small parrots appreciate human companionship or that of their own species just as much as

the larger ones. Most small parrots are highly sociable. Whether or not they are tame, they will appreciate a companion of their own kind— preferably acquired at the same time or soon after. Only the purchaser of a hand-reared bird who can spend much time with this parrot daily should consider buying a single pet. A small parrot's behavior is usually more interesting to observe when it can interact with others. There is no sadder sight than a single lovebird or parrotlet left alone for long hours.

Bearing these facts in mind, the first decision is whether to buy a single bird or two. If you buy a pair, will you want to breed from them? Some owners are not happy to part with the young, especially if the market for that species is saturated. Many small parrots are inexpensive and prolific; when their value is low it might be difficult to find homes where their quality of life will not be in doubt. You might find it difficult to part with the young from a sentimental point of view, but there is a limit to the number you can care for in a manner that meets a good standard. Therefore, you must be clear from the start what your purpose is.

In most species two males will live together happily. Two females might be compatible unless the species is a female-dominant one,

Opposite: *Lovebirds appreciate companions of their own species.*

like a lovebird or a *Poicephalus* parrot such as a Senegal or a Meyer's.

Sexing some species is almost impossible by outward appearance and even by behavior. Today, all parrots in aviculture can be sexed using DNA technology. A few feathers or a drop of blood are sent to an avian diagnostic laboratory and the bird's sex is revealed. This procedure is less often carried out with species of low monetary value as sexing might cost nearly as much as the value of the bird. Purchasers of two lovebirds usually take a chance on their being of the desired sex.

If you are looking for a fairly inexpensive single companion of a small species, among the most suitable, if hand-reared, are *Pyrrhura* conures such as the Green-cheeked and the Maroon-bellied (Red-bellied), parrotlets (*Forpus* species) and Lineolated and Quaker Parakeets. Conures and Quakers are long-tailed birds with plenty of character. It is unusual for the small conures to learn to mimic; in contrast, Quakers can be excellent "talkers." They also have loud voices! Some hand-reared Quakers and conures that receive lots of attention do not exceed a noise level that is tolerable. Remember, however, that unless you keep the little Lineolated Parakeets, you can expect your parrot to be loud at times. This point should be considered carefully because it can cause problems with other family members and neighbors.

Similar in body size, at about 10 inches (25 cm) including the tail, and considerably more expensive, are the short-tailed true parrots: caiques, *Poicephalus*, and *Pionus* parrots. Caiques are the clownish extroverts of the parrot world, endlessly amusing—and very strong-willed. They have quite piercing yaps and whistles. *Pionus*, such as Maximilian's, are more laid-back and less shrill. Both kinds are capable of amusing themselves and *Pionus* are less demanding than the larger parrots.

If you are out for most of the day you should already have questioned whether a parrot is right for you. It is asking for trouble to obtain a Gray Parrot, for example, in these circumstances. One lady contacted me regarding a six-month-old Gray Parrot that was plucking itself. I guessed immediately that it was left alone all day. A hand-reared bird that has known nothing but human companionship feels insecure when it is abandoned for long hours.

When making a choice, it is important to give consideration to the type of household in which the parrot will live. Parrots and small children are seldom a good combination. Whether older children can live with a parrot without causing it problems by teasing it will depend very much on the attitude of the parents and whether they have taught their children to show respect to animals.

In assessing which species are suitable for families with small children, I've taken into account:

- The size of the species and how serious an injury it could cause.
- How sensitive it is and the effect that teasing will have on it. (This is not to infer that any bird

Left: A child that respects household pets should have no problem getting along with a parrot.

is insensitive to teasing, but that a Gray Parrot, for example, will be more stressed by this than a caique.) This should be taken as a guide as there is much individual variation in character.

• How disturbing it will find the quick and unpredictable movements of small children.

Knowledge of the characteristics of the different types are useful, but parrots are highly individualistic, so generalizations are not always accurate. The following table (see below) should be taken as a guide only. There will be many exceptions.

Suitability as family pets

SPECIES	FAMILY WITH SMALL CHILDREN	FAMILY WITH OLDER CHILDREN
Amazon	no	yes
Budgerigar	yes	yes
Caique	no	possibly
Cockatiel	yes	yes
Cockatoo (white)	no	possibly
Conures, *Aratinga*	no	yes
Conures, *Pyrrhura*	yes	yes
Gray Parrot	no	yes
Lorikeet, Green-naped and Swainson's/Rainbow	yes possibly	yes yes
Lovebird	possibly	yes
Macaw (large)	no	possibly
Parrotlet	yes	yes
Pionus parrots (Maximilian's, etc)	yes	female only
Senegal Parrot and other small *Poicephalus*	no	possibly

AMAZON PARROTS

Amazon parrots have been popular pets for centuries, since the 16th-century reign of Queen Elizabeth I. They owe their popularity to their beauty, intelligence, and ability to mimic. They vary greatly in temperament and character according to species, age, and sex. The most popular are the Blue-fronted Amazon (*Amazona aestiva*), the Yellow-crowned Amazon (*Amazona ochrocephala ochrocephala*), the Double Yellow-head Amazon (*Amazona oratrix*), and, where available, the Yellow-naped Amazon (*Amazona auropalliata*).

These Amazons are excellent mimics and entertainers with a happy temperament. Singing and laughing half the day and responding enthusiastically to music, it would be difficult to find a better companion. Feather plucking is rare, indicating a temperament that can cope with stress. However, some are rather noisy birds. Males, especially, have an excitable temperament. Those seeking a pet of these species are advised to purchase a DNA-sexed female. When adult, few male Double Yellow-heads are considered safe family pets during the breeding season.

The gentle disposition and big, appealing eyes of the Mealy Amazon (*Amazona farinosa*) long ago made it one of my favorite Amazon parrots. Sadly still legally imported by the hundreds from Guyana into Europe and South Africa, it is one of the Amazons least appreciated by birdkeepers, and also one of the loudest.

Amazona amazonica
ORANGE-WINGED AMAZON

This is one of the least expensive Amazons in North America, due to the fact that large numbers of wild-caught birds were once legally imported. (This is now prohibited under the Wild Bird Conservation Act of 1992.) Elsewhere, any offered at low prices, not tame, and/or with a narrow open ring are wild-caught birds. Captive-bred, hand-reared Orange-winged Amazons should wear a closed ring, and they will be tame, confiding, and higher-priced.

Orange-winged Amazon

Blue-fronted Amazon

Amazona o. ochrocephala
YELLOW-CROWNED AMAZON

Also known as Yellow-fronted Amazon

The Wild Bird Conservation Act of 1992 means that North Americans can no longer import wild-caught Yellow-crowned Amazon parrots, though captive-bred birds are still available. They have wonderful personalities, are good mimics, and are endlessly entertaining, with a real zest for life! This applies to all the Amazon parrots with yellow on their heads. I have shared my life with a female for 38 years.

Amazona aestiva
BLUE-FRONTED AMAZON

Distinguished from the Orange-winged Amazon by its black beak and larger size, the Blue-fronted Amazon has a more volatile temperament. However, this is a very handsome bird, loaded with personality. Most of those available are the *xanthopteryx* sub-species, many of which have a large area of yellow at the bend of the wing. In contrast, the nominate race from Brazil (rarely available these days) has red in this area.

Yellow-crowned Amazon

Melopsittacus undulatus
BUDGERIGAR

Before a range of parrots was available, the popularity of the "budgie" was huge—and rightly so. Acquired when young, they make excellent pets. The older birds, often found in pet stores, are suitable only for an aviary and will never become tame. Make the effort to find a breeder and acquire a young bird that is 5 or 6 weeks old. You can distinguish a young bird by the pale color of the cere, the dark eyes, and barring on the forehead that extends to the cere (some mutations such as albino and lutino lack barring).

You can sex young birds of most colors according to the color of the cere, but many pet store staff are unaware of this. In the main varieties of Budgerigar, such as green and blue, the cere is pink or purple in a young male and light blue, usually with the area around the nostrils being white, in a young female. Adult females not in breeding condition might have a light blue cere, distinguished easily from the rich blue of an adult male. In adult males of the red-eyed mutations (lutino and albino) and in some pieds, the cere might remain the purple color of a young bird. Males are invariably better mimics than females, but the color of their plumage has no relevance to talking ability.

Budgerigar

CAIQUES
(PIONITES)

These alert little parrots conceal a personality as big as that of a macaw in spite of their small size. When feeling aggressive they can fight an Amazon, yet they are so sociable that they will cuddle up to a cockatoo if they need a companion. Caiques are bundles of fun that love to play and explore. They can be hilariously amusing little show-offs. Their fascinating behavior and their small size make them ideal subjects for the home, but because they are so full of mischief they must never be left unattended when outside their cage as they can get into all kinds of trouble.

A couple of hand-reared youngsters could be the ideal choice for someone who is out of the house for hours every day. Caiques do have faults, though: they have shrill calls and a propensity to nip if they do not get their way. Their change in temperament can also be sudden: they can cuddle one moment and nip the next.

Pionites melanocephala
BLACK-HEADED CAIQUE

The Black-headed Caique is readily available at a reasonable price.

Pionites leucogaster
WHITE-BELLIED CAIQUE

The White-bellied Caique is less common, but is equally enjoyable.

Black-headed Caique

White-bellied Caiques

Nymphicus hollandicus
COCKATIEL

The Cockatiel can make a wonderful pet and is an excellent species for a beginner. Before buying one, listen to the shrill voice of an adult.

The diet of a Cockatiel is less complicated than that of larger parrots, so dietary deficiencies are unlikely to occur. A male will make the best talker and can acquire a large vocabulary, but it is very difficult for an inexperienced person to distinguish a male in nest feather. A number of color mutations are available. There are problems with some females who lay excessive numbers of eggs despite lacking a partner.

Cockatiels

COCKATOOS
(CACATUA)

Hand-reared cockatoos are so affectionate and appealing that some inexperienced people buy them on impulse, unaware of the commitment involved and the lifestyle that can accommodate this commitment.

Breeders of white cockatoos compound these difficulties by selling the young cockatoos at 14 to 16 weeks and mislead prospective buyers into believing they have weaned the cockatoo when this could only be true in the case of a Bare-eyed Cockatoo (*Cacatua sanguinea*)—a species that attains independence at an earlier age. Most breeders force young white cockatoos to eat on their own before they are physically and emotionally ready to do so. Worse still, many sell them with instructions to give them hard foods such as seeds or pellets. Cockatoos need soft foods for many weeks, and, in most cases, owners also need to spoon-feed them until they are at least 20 weeks old.

New cockatoo owners rarely recognize the signs of hunger, but are frequently advised not to hand-feed their young cockatoo. On the contrary, you should spoon-feed every young cockatoo until it is no longer interested in this procedure.

Parent-reared young cockatoos that are accustomed to people at an early age, or those that have been hand-reared with minimum human contact, ultimately make better pets because they are less dependent on people. Many hand-reared cockatoos are often confused about their identity and have an abnormally strong craving to be with people: they are psychologically maladjusted and incapable of living normal lives.

There is another aspect of white cockatoos that makes these birds quite difficult to live with. They have powder-down feathers that grow continuously, and these feathers give off white powder that protects and cleans the feathers. White cockatoos give off more of this powder than other parrots; a cloud of white dust escapes when they ruffle their feathers. This can adversely affect the health of asthma and allergy sufferers. It is very important to spray a white cockatoo three or four times a week or even to take it into the shower. This helps to prevent a buildup of feather dust.

Forced weaning has profound psychological effects on white cockatoos. It makes them exceedingly anxious and clingy. They will pluck their feathers and fling seeds. They are unable to eat enough hard food to sustain themselves and are disinclined to feed on their own. Hungry young cockatoos will whine to be fed and scream for attention. Only after you have spoon-fed them will they be interested in trying foods you place before them on their own.

The Greater Sulfur-crested Cockatoo (*Cacatua galerita*) is, in my opinion, one of the most intelligent of all birds, but needs a special kind of owner who understands its psychological needs and who can give it an endless supply of items, particularly for gnawing, to keep it occupied. This is a large, powerful bird, and one that needs plenty of space. Most captive birds are kept in aviaries or cages that are much too small. They love to walk around on the ground, to dig, and to play. It is important to provide a stimulating environment to allow them to do so. As a flock species, they have a desperate need for companions of their own kind.

Left: Umbrella Cockatoo **Right**: Moluccan Cockatoo

CONURES (*ARATINGA* AND *PYRRHURA*)

There are two genera (groups) of conures that are popular with bird keepers: *Aratinga* and *Pyrrhura*. Basically green, most of them have attractive plumage and personalities to match. The larger *Aratinga* are often amusing characters, more like parrots than parakeets, but they have one serious disadvantage—their loud, harsh voices. Some, such as the Sun Conure, are so colorful that they are subjects of impulse buying, and potential owners tend to ignore the warnings on their vocal capabilities—be sure you first hear the call of an adult bird before you consider a purchase. Only acquire young, hand-reared birds as companions.

Aratinga solstitialis
SUN CONURE

The Sun Conure has a brilliant plumage in shades of yellow, vibrant orange, and green. It is outstandingly beautiful by any standards. Jim Hayward, a well-known breeder in the United Kingdom, once wrote of his aviary birds: "Sun Conures are at their most spectacular when the orb of the sun is beginning to sink below the horizon; then, as they are bathed in the orange light, they take on a fiery glow."

The intensity of color varies in individuals, but most do not need any help from the sunset! Sun Conures are often rehomed because their loud voices indoors are intolerable.

Aratinga jandaya
JENDAYA CONURE

The Jendaya and Golden-capped Conure (*Aratinga auricapilla*) are closely related. They have much more green in their plumage than the Sun Conure and equally loud voices. All three species measure about 12 inches (30 cm) and weigh about 4 ounces (120 g).

Sun Conure

Jendaya Conure

Golden-crowned Conure

Mitred Conure

Another group of *Aratinga* is green with scarlet markings on the head and on the bend of the wing. They are larger, with personalities that are more like those of the larger parrots. If obtained when young, identification can cause confusion. They make exceptionally affectionate and intelligent companions, being playful and inquisitive. The big question: can you stand the noise?

Aratinga mitrata
MITRED CONURE

North Americans can no longer import wild-caught birds; however, breeders still breed the species. Note that some unscrupulous dealers cut off the tails and sell the birds as Amazons to uninformed people. The adult is scarlet on the forehead and lores with patches or flecks of red on the cheeks and ear coverts. The young bird has a dark-red forehead, except for the odd red feather on its head, and is not to be confused with Wagler's Conure.

Aratinga wagleri wagleri
WAGLER'S CONURE

Wagler's Conure is larger than the Mitred Conure with more red on the bend of its wing. Its forehead, upper part of its lores, and forepart of its crown are red. Young birds are dull red on the forehead.

Aratinga erythrogenys
RED-MASKED CONURE

Also known as the Cherry-headed Conure

The Red-masked Conure is rare in the wild due to overtrapping in Ecuador and Peru. The adults have an unbroken area of red from their forehead to the rear of their crown. Their lores and cheeks are also red. Young birds have a narrow line of brown on their forehead.

There are several small species of *Aratinga* conures that are seldom kept as pets outside the United States. They include the Peach-fronted (or Golden-crowned, *Aratinga aurea*) and the Orange-fronted, Petz's, or Half-moon Conure. The Peach-fronted has a black beak and a circle of orange feathers surrounding the eye, whereas the Orange-fronted has an ivory-colored upper mandible (the lower mandible is black). These two species are mainly green, measure about 10 inches (25 cm) and weigh about 3 ounces (75 g).

Very closely related to the *Aratinga* conures, the Nanday Conure (*Nendayus nanday*) is distinguished by its mainly black head. Despite its loud voice, hand-reared birds are quite popular as pets. One of the largest and most beautiful of the conures is the Lesser Patagonian (*Cyanoliseus patagonus patagonus*). It has a gentle temperament and hand-reared birds are very sweet. Unfortunately, they are very loud.

Closely related to the conures is the Quaker, or Monk, Parakeet (*Myiopsitta monachus*). Hand-reared birds are great favorites as pets, and some become talented mimics. Again, their only fault is their loud voice, but this is less of a problem with hand-reared birds that receive lots of attention.

Red-masked Conure

Eclectus polychloros
ECLECTUS PARROTS

The vibrant colors and unique hairlike plumage on the head and underparts of Eclectus Parrots invariably attract bird lovers. This species shows the most extreme sexual dimorphism of any member of the parrot family: the male is bright green and the female is red and blue or mauve (or just red). A male and female sitting side by side is one of the most memorable sights in the avian kingdom, except that they rarely do sit together. Eclectus belong to a large group of parrots in which the males have orange or red bills and the female's beaks are black or of a neutral shade.

Also in this group are Muller's Parrots (*Tanygnathus sumatranus*), and *Psittacula* parakeets such as the Ringneck Parakeet. All these are female-dominant, and only the Ringneck Parakeet is commonly kept as a pet. The pair bond hardly exists or is nonexistent. It is probable that in the wild a female selects a new mate every season. The males first have to overcome their fear of the female and become increasingly bold when they come into breeding condition. The male's bill plays a role in courtship. An Eclectus Parrot, for example, courts the female by vigorously tapping his beak against the female's, and, in *Psittacula* parakeets, head-swirling and courtship feeding

Blue-rumped Parrots

Eclectus Parrots—female left, male right

Ringneck Parakeet

play a big role. The red bill thrust in her face probably acts as some kind of stimulant to the female. There is little affectionate behavior and mutual preening is rare.

As already mentioned, female Eclectus Parrots are dominant and they are also of uncertain temper. If they are hand-reared they can make good pets until they become sexually mature, which takes place at about the age of three. After this age their behavior is likely to be erratic.

It is not in a female's nature to bond closely with a male in the wild; therefore, when kept as a pet she will not normally form a strong bond with a human. Anyone who wants an affectionate companion should choose either a male or a different species. Males are more gentle and loving and can make wonderful pets. However, they are sensitive birds and both males and females pluck themselves if stressed. They can be good mimics and can also be consistently loud.

Gray Parrot

Psittacus erithacus
GRAY PARROT

Gray Parrots are so famous for their ability to mimic that the problems that occur in probably two out of three Grays are ignored when the choice of species is made. The problems are not the fault of the individual bird but originate from its sensitive and highly intelligent nature, which calls for special care in a captive situation. This is not a gray-colored version of an Amazon parrot, for example, but a very observant thinker that reacts to every nuance of behavior and to the smallest alteration in the environment. This helps to explain why the incidence of feather plucking is higher in Grays than in any other species: feather plucking is most often caused by stress. Apart from the ability to mimic, which is most marked in Grays that have a strong bond with their owner, they are noted for their quiet and nonaggressive demeanor. Their diet needs special attention (see Chapter 8) if they are to survive more than a decade. Grays are suitable only for people who can offer a lot of time and thought to keeping them happy and healthy.

The Timneh Gray subspecies (*Psittacus eritha-cus timneh*) is recognized by its slightly smaller size and dark-red or slaty-red tail. (In young birds the tail is mainly dark gray.) The undertail coverts are tinged dark gray with red, not scarlet, as in the nominate race. The beak is distinctive in adults: orange-brown in the center of the upper mandible, elsewhere black. The upper mandible is mainly brown in young birds. The upper parts are dark, as are the ear coverts; the head feathers are margined with gray. Timneh Grays are less popular (reflected in their low selling price) only because their tails are not scarlet. They are excellent mimics, and, in fact, might make even better pets because behavioral problems such as feather plucking seem to be less common.

Some people think that the yellow eyes of Gray Parrots give them an untrustworthy appearance. It must be said that many Grays delight in nipping, first gaining a person's trust by lowering their heads to be scratched! However, the intelligence of this species, which is sometimes apparent due to its ability to mimic words and to use them appropriately, will give endless amusement.

Young Timneh Grays

Deroptyus accipitrinus
HAWK-HEADED PARROT

Hawk-headed Parrots are extraordinary. When young they are so appealing that they might tempt impulse buyers. When adult (at about 3 years) their extreme aggressiveness makes them difficult to live with. Everything about this unique and beautiful parrot is designed to intimidate. When it is sitting quietly it does not look very threatening, but its demeanor can change in an instant. This sudden change occurs when the bird throws up its head fan of red and blue feathers, half opens its wings, and puffs out its body feathers. The apparent increase in size is accompanied by hissing and swaying.

In some species, aggression is just bluffing. Not so with these parrots! Hand-reared Hawk-headeds know no fear of humans. They don't just attack. They cling onto an ear if one is uncovered, or to a hand. One man ended up in the hospital as a result, needing stitches in his hand. I would not recommend hand-rearing or suggest that this species makes a suitable pet. It can also be aggressive toward other pet birds in the home. One I know of attacked an unsuspecting Blue and Yellow Macaw (with which it had lived for months) and bit it through the tongue.

Hawk-headed Parrot

LORIES AND LORIKEETS

While they might learn to imitate a few words in a small voice, it is not talking ability that endears lorikeets to parrot lovers. The outstanding attributes of these brush-tongued parrots are their beauty, playfulness, inquisitive behavior, and capacity for great affection toward human companions and those of their own kind. What joy to watch them rolling around on the cage floor in play, or locked in a friendly tussle with a companion. They take a keen interest in everything, usually wanting to investigate. Unlike other birds, this means testing with the tongue. One then has the pleasure of observing the tiny papillae, or brushes, at the tip.

Rainbow Lorikeets

Green-naped Lorikeet

The personality varies greatly according to the species; there are 53 species but only a small number are well known. They are great fun to keep because they are so active, and also inventive in their play. They don't sit around most of the day doing nothing. However, they have serious disadvantages when kept in the home. Most species are noisy and some have piercing calls. They can be extremely aggressive toward other birds. They also need a lot of exercise; if they are confined to a cage they will become overweight and bored, leading to screaming sessions. Their liquid droppings are squirted all over the place and they flick tiny pieces

Musk Lorikeet

Little Lorikeets

of fruit that stick to the cage and surroundings, making them too messy for most households. It takes a special person to look after a lorikeet indoors. Because they are so inquisitive and like to get into small spaces, any such spaces (perhaps behind a fireplace) must be blocked up. Constant vigilance is necessary. A much-loved Green-naped Lorikeet died when it fell into the toilet.

One of the many subspecies of *Trichoglossus haematodus* is ideal for the beginner. In the United States and Europe this will usually be the Green-naped Lorikeet (*T.h. haematodus*). There are 20 more, though most are not common in captivity. If available, they make equally good pets if acquired when young, and hand-reared. The smaller Musk Lorikeet (*Glossopsitta concinna*) is also sometimes kept as a pet in Australia and New Zealand. The Little Lorikeet (*Glossopsitta pusilla*) is not available outside Australia, but some Australians describe these tiny birds as enchanting pets.

There are 11 genera of lories, but members of only two are commonly kept as pets. Lories are the short-tailed, heavier-bodied equivalent of the long-tailed lorikeets. They can be very loud, and, since most species are larger than lorikeets, their liquid droppings are copious; these two facts mean that it is not practical to keep them indoors. Nevertheless, quite a lot are hand-reared and sold into the pet trade. All too often they become unwanted, or their lives are short because they are incorrectly fed. Nevertheless, in caring and responsible hands, certain species can make very affectionate pets. The Yellow-backed and Chattering Lories (*Lorius garrulus garrulus* and *L.g. flavopalliatus*) and the Black-capped (*Lorius lory*) often become talented mimics. They have strong personalities and are highly intelligent. The same applies to the Red Lory (*Eos bornea*). However, these species have become much rarer and are now seldom kept as pets.

Chattering Lory

Red Lory

Black-capped Lory

Peach-faced Lovebirds

LOVEBIRDS

Some hand-reared lovebirds make good pets, but the potential of individuals is difficult to evaluate when they are young. Also, they must be handled daily to keep them tame, thus a single bird should not be obtained by someone without the time to devote to it. In any case, lovebirds are happiest when kept in pairs.

There are nine species, of which the Peach-faced (*Agapornis roseicollis*), sometimes called Rosy-faced, is the most common and the most likely to be hand-reared as a pet. Its popularity has led to its being available in countless color mutations. One of the most attractive is the lutino—yellow with a contrasting pink face. In this species, male and female can be determined only by behavior or by DNA sexing. I once went into a pet store and was asked if I could sex a

"pair" of lovebirds. They turned out to be a pied mutation of a Peach-faced and Masked Lovebird. The store owner was convinced they were a pair because they sat together all the time and seemed so attached to each other. A fairly conclusive method of sexing a Peach-faced Lovebird is to give it some fresh-cut twigs of willow. If it strips the bark and twigs, and tucks them into the feathers of the rump and back, it is a female. If there is a nest-box available, she will carry the willow inside.

In the Netherlands, Ellen Karhausen keeps four lovebirds (wing-clipped) who travel everywhere with her, even riding on her bicycle. She says: "There are many hazards in the house because lovebirds are so curious, exploring holes and any objects they can enter. This could result in them being stuck or drowned. However, the more you let them out, the less they think of their cage as a nest and the less they will try to defend it by nipping you."

MACAWS

The smaller macaws might not have the glamor of a Scarlet or the panache of a Blue and Yellow, but they have huge personalities in those little frames. They are, in fact, a much more sensible alternative for the average household, being less destructive, less noisy, and of a size that anyone can handle. Vivacious, intelligent, and playful, they have great appeal to the lover of neotropical parrots.

There are six species, all from South America, varying in size from 12 inches (30 cm) in Hahn's and Noble Macaws (*Diopsittaca nobilis nobilis* and *D.n. cumanensis*) to the 19-inch (49 cm) Severe (*Ara severa*) and Blue-headed Macaws (*Propyrrhura couloni*) that are only half the length of their more charismatic counterparts. All are green with touches of color on the head and wings. The lores and area around the eye are bare of feathers, the bare area being smallest in *nobilis* and largest in the Severe Macaw. They have pleasing outlines, with shorter tails in proportion to the body than those of the large macaws. Active and inquisitive, these birds appreciate a large cage with interesting objects to explore, ropes on which to play, and the provision of fresh-cut branches (willow, elm, or

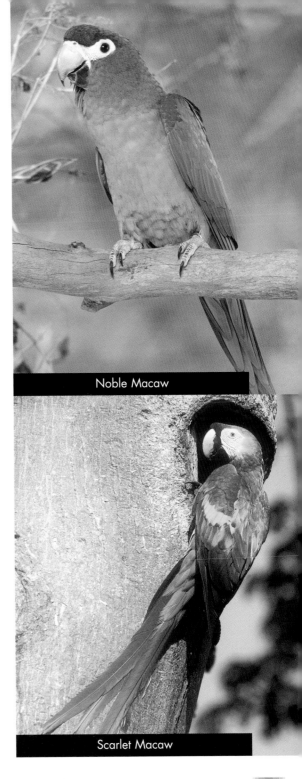

Noble Macaw

Scarlet Macaw

apple) at regular intervals. The small macaws, with the possible exception of Red-bellied (*Orthopsittaca manilata*), are always alert and interested in what is going on around them.

Distinctive and small, the Red-bellied Macaw differs in both behavior and temperament. Though the Wild Bird Conservation Act of 1992 prohibits it from being imported to North America, it is unfortunately still being imported elsewhere. The price is low and it attracts part-time dealers who hike up the price and advertise the birds in local papers, describing them only as "macaws." This attracts the uninitiated. Its nervous temperament, susceptibility to obesity, and degenerative changes in the heart result in a short lifespan in captivity. It is definitely not to be recommended as a pet. Usually isolated and sold individually, these unfortunate birds lead sad and stressful lives—and usually very brief ones.

The Noble (and Hahn's) Macaws are closely related to the *Aratinga* conures. Again they often sell merely because they were named macaws, although, for all practical purposes, they can be treated as conures. Hahn's Macaw is the best-known and least expensive member

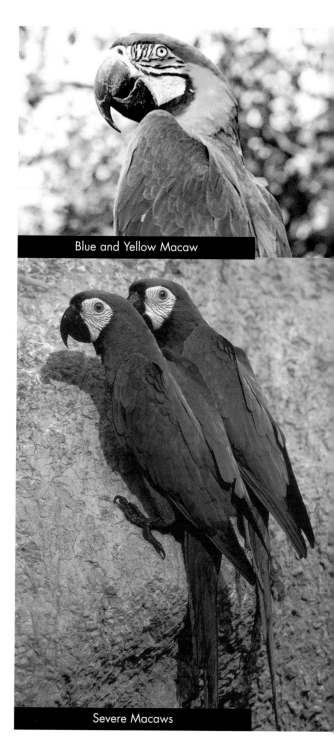

Blue and Yellow Macaw

Severe Macaws

Blue-headed Macaw

of the group. Some birds are noisy, and this may be because they lack stimulation or need more attention. The Noble Macaw is less often available. The Yellow-collared Macaw has good pet potential and can learn to mimic a few words. I have a great affection for this species, which is cheeky and playful. Illiger's Macaw (*Propyrrhura maracana*) is on Appendix I of CITES, scarcer, and higher-priced, but its pet potential is just as good as that of the Yellow-collared. The Severe, or Chestnut-fronted, Macaw is often kept as a pet in the United States but seldom elsewhere. Finally, there is the Blue-headed, or Coulon's, Macaw (*Propyrrhura couloni*). It is too rare to be kept as a pet, although this situation is rapidly changing in Eastern Europe, where it is more frequently bred.

The large macaws are a different proposition altogether. They are not normally suitable as pets except perhaps for the house-bound, who can lavish hours of attention on them daily.

Sadly, many people who know little or nothing about parrots buy a macaw as a sort of flamboyant accessory or as a status symbol. This is very sad, given that a large macaw demands as much attention as a child. If it does

Red-bellied Macaws

not receive it, its screaming or biting will result in it being rehomed after a short time. If it has not been with sensitive and caring people from the very start, behavioral problems will emerge that might be very difficult to reverse. There are highly practical reasons why the large macaws are not suited to life in the home: they are extremely loud and their destructiveness can make a chainsaw look feeble! Their beaks have enormous power and can cause serious injury. They know this, and some macaws take delight in threatening people (perhaps laughing maniacally at the same time!). When macaws become excited they tend to lunge at people; this can be intimidating. On the other hand they can be sweet and affectionate, but their moods can change with frightening rapidity. It takes a very special kind of birdkeeper to give macaws the quality of life that they need and deserve.

Macaws are special birds—highly intelligent and sensitive. They are also very large, very loud, destructive, and expensive to keep well. They are extremely long-lived. If well cared for they can survive into their 50s, by which age they will probably be showing signs of arthritis and cataracts.

I have rarely seen large macaws kept indoors in conditions that seemed satisfactory. Lucky are the few macaws kept like Oscar. He has the best of both worlds: a family to interact with during evenings and weekends and an outdoor aviary right outside the kitchen where he can fly and play when the family members are absent.

PARAKEETS

Most parakeets thrive better in an aviary than in a home, because they need a lot of flying exercise. Despite this, parakeets are sometimes hand-reared as pets. Some breeders hand-rear species that are normally only suitable for aviaries, including Australian parakeets and Kakarikis (New Zealand parakeets). They do so because overproduction makes it difficult to sell parent-reared birds and the uninitiated believe that

Moustache Parakeet

any hand-reared member of the parrot family will make a good pet. Hand-reared Australian and New Zealand parakeets need more flying exercise than is possible in most homes, and, equally important, usually become aggressive and spiteful when mature.

Indian Ringneck Parakeets (*Psittacula krameri manillensis*) are so numerous and low-priced that they are often bought without due consideration and ultimately are given away or even released. Although they are not usually considered ideal birds for the home, some make good pets if hand-reared. They are intelligent, cheeky, and might become good mimics. One owner of a male described his vocabulary as "amazing," a repertoire that he repeated for minutes at a time and an astonishing ability to say things in the correct context. This might be achieved only in a hand-reared bird acquired when very young. The plumage does not indicate the sex until the age of 2 years, and I would suggest DNA sexing before purchase as males are likely to make the best pets and the best mimics. On the other hand, one owner of a female Moustache Parakeet (*Psittacula alexandri*) recorded that she was a good talker. Furthermore, she had remained tame and friendly despite rearing many chicks. Her

Orange-fronted Conures

ability to mimic was inherited by her young, who started to talk at an early age.

Most parakeets from South America have much better temperaments as pets than those from the Old World. Conures and Quakers have already been mentioned. There are many other species, whose availability is greatly reduced since their importation diminished or stopped. Examples are the little parakeets of the genus *Brotogeris*.

Hand-reared Orange-flanked (*B. pyrrhopterus*) Parakeets make enchanting little companions. However, because they are difficult to breed in captivity, they are seldom available. The pet potential of hand-reared members of the genus *Bolborhynchus* is unrecorded. I can vouch for the fact that a parent-reared male Mountain Parakeet (*B. aurifrons*) has made a wonderful companion for a friend. She described him as follows: "He's a very good pet bird, a gentle character, generally with a quiet voice, although he does call out loudly when he's watching out for wild birds! He learned to say a few words and to whistle by copying my Celestial Parrotlet. He became tame very easily, copying the parrotlet in stepping onto my finger. He likes to cuddle up to me in the evenings and enjoys having his chin scratched. He is independent in character and explores his surroundings, but when he feels threatened he spreads his wings out, lowers his head and growls!"

The same pet potential might be true of the Lineolated Parakeet (*B. lineola*). Many different color mutations of the latter are now available, including blue and lutino. Their tiny size and small voices could make them the perfect apartment pets.

Mountain Parakeet

Lineolated Parakeets

Green-rumped Parrotlet

PARROTLETS

True miniature parrots, not unlike Amazons in shape, the *Forpus* parrotlets measure only about 5 inches (13 cm) long and weigh about ¾ to 1 ounce (22 to 30 g). Hand-reared birds can remain tame, learn to talk, and make excellent pets for those who don't have the space or the time for a larger parrot. However, this is not to infer that they do not need lots of attention. They do if they are to remain tame and contented. Like many small parrots, they have big personalities and minds of their own. They can be very strong-willed. A pair can be quite aggressive toward each other—when kept in a cage they need space. The best known is the Celestial, or Pacific, Parrotlet (*Forpus coelestis*). Parrotlets are very popular, and more species are readily available. Among these are the Green-rumped (*Forpus passerinus*), the Mexican Parrotlet (*Forpus cyanopygius*), and the Spectacled Parrotlet (*Forpus conspicillatus*).

My friend with the Mountain Parakeet described her Celestial Parrotlet as follows: "He was the tamest bird I have ever had and he was very bonded to me. The only downside was his very jealous and occasionally vicious temperament, which I gather is typical of Celestial Parrotlets. He drew blood on various occasions. However, he was a brilliant talker and whistler in a little birdie voice! He was very funny to be with and such a cuddly character!"

Spengel's Parrotlets

Celestial Parrotlet

PIONUS PARROTS

The *Pionus* are the only neotropical parrots with red undertail coverts. Of quite heavy build, they have short, wide tails and range in size from 9 inches (24 cm) to 11 inches (28 cm); they weigh between 6¼ and 9½ ounces (180 and 270 g). In some respects they are closest in behavior and needs to Amazon parrots, but their personalities are usually less excitable. They are not as loud (although some *Pionus* can be quite noisy at times) and their range of plumage colors is interesting. There is a more important advantage: they are less demanding and well able to keep themselves amused without frequently calling for attention. That does not mean, however, that they should not have a couple of regular periods of

Blue-headed Pionus

Maximilian's Pionus

interaction daily with their human friends. They are seldom talented mimics, although a few individuals are good "talkers." Tame *Pionus* love to have their heads scratched, but seldom accept any other kind of contact. It should be noted that, when mature, some males become very aggressive and territorial.

Until the early 1970s only the Blue-headed Pionus (*Pionus menstruus*) was well known. It was not until the early 1980s that White-capped and Maximilian's became available. Smaller numbers of Bronze-winged and Dusky were imported. Trade in the other two members of the genus, the Coral-billed and the Plum-crowned, has always been small. In wild-caught Dusky Pionus, mortality is extremely high and most birds die within six months. I would appeal to parrot lovers not to buy wild-caught birds, if not for ethical reasons, then because they are a disease risk to your other birds (and to you, as many suffer from psittacosis).

The species that are imported are all available from breeders if you have the time and patience to search for them. More Maximilian's are bred than any other *Pionus*, with smaller numbers of Blue-headed Pionus, Bronze-winged, and White-capped. I would not recommend Bronze-winged Pionus as pets due to their highly nervous temperament. This sometimes manifests itself in times of stress as rapid, wheezy breathing that is similar to the symptoms of respiratory disease, to which *Pionus* are very susceptible.

One owner of a male and a female White-capped Pionus described the male as more excitable, very loving, tolerant of everyone, and with a vocabulary of about 30 words. In marked contrast, the female was very quiet, more aloof, and with a smaller vocabulary. This could apply to any species of *Pionus*. My preference would be for a female as mature males usually become aggressive when in breeding condition.

White-capped Pionus

SENEGAL PARROTS AND OTHER *POICEPHALUS*

Africa has a genus of small short-tailed parrots—the *Poicephalus*. These small parrots make ideal pets for someone who lives alone and keeps the bird confined to its cage when visitors arrive. In this scenario they can be devoted and affectionate.

The best known are the Senegal and the Meyer's. The Red-bellied has similar behavior and temperament, and the males, with their orange breasts, are very beautiful.

Meyer's Parrot

Senegal Parrot

The Wild Bird Conservation Act of 1992 means that North Americans can no longer import wild-caught Senegals, though it is still allowed elsewhere. Regrettably, this often tempts people who have no knowledge of parrots to buy them. Most wild-caught Senegals are extremely nervous; adult birds never become tame and show intense fear of humans. It is cruel to keep them closely confined in a cage. Only in a spacious aviary will they become less fearful.

Some hand-reared birds make enchanting pets, especially when young. Others are quite difficult for anyone but the most experienced parrot owners, being aggressive toward people and other pets. They need much attention and frequent handling. Becoming very nippy for an extended period at about 2 years of age is not unusual. However, the most vital information about the small *Poicephalus* is that they are not suitable as family pets. They will usually form a strong bond with one person and ward off everyone else with behavior that could be described as vicious. A female Red-bellied Parrot I know has acquired a large vocabulary; she quickly learns new words, puts the cat firmly in its place, and rides on the children's toy cars. However, it is the man of the household who is her favorite, and she has been known to nip other family members. With the youngest child she was gentle while he was under 1 year old, as though aware of his vulnerability, but her behavior changed when he grew older.

Red-bellied Parrot

Females are dominant. On no account must two adult females be kept together: one will either kill the other or cause it so much stress that it dies. However, the best are wonderful pets.

The Brown-headed (*P. cryptoxanthus*) is the least colorful but has perhaps the sweetest temperament. The two larger members of the genus, Jardine's (*P. gulielmi*) and the larger and less-available Gray-headed Parrot (*P. fuscicollis*), are generally more gentle than their smaller cousins and can make enchanting pets. I believe that the Gray-headed Parrot, with its large beak and attractive whistling calls, is a highly underrated species as a companion. However, it is not well known and availability is not good in North America and elsewhere in the world.

Brown-headed Parrot

Jardine's Parrot

3

What you need and where to buy it

Before you buy a parrot, plan your expenditure. The cage and accessories can cost more than the parrot. Resist the temptation to buy a cheap cage for an inexpensive bird. The cage will be its home for many years, so do a little research on the types available and the most suitable cage for the species. If you have yet to make up your mind about the species, do not buy the cage first!

To set up the cage and accessories, you can either visit a large pet store or specialist parrot center, or you can order everything online. I would recommend seeing what you are buying, because quality is not necessarily apparent from a web page or catalog. This is especially important with the cage. It is wise to buy from a center that has a good product range.

Opposite: *A rope perch can be obtained from a pet store.*

CAGES

A parrot needs a spacious, good-quality cage—an expensive item. Don't buy an inexpensive cage and tell yourself that you will buy a better one when you can afford it. Small cages can cause behavioral problems such as aggression, and cheap cages could be made of metals with toxic elements. Also, parrots can become very attached to their cages and will not appreciate a change. Do not buy a second-hand cage unless you are certain that the previous occupant did not die of an infectious disease. In any case, if the cage is second-hand, clean it thoroughly and disinfect it with an agent that kills viruses.

There are many different cages available, so you might have a problem choosing one. For smaller cages, eliminate those that are higher than they are wide, as a parrot needs to be able to fly or jump from perch to perch. Except for the long-tailed macaws, width is more important than height. Look at the bars of the cage. Some bars should be horizontal, not vertical; this permits your parrot to climb around more easily.

Look for a cage on casters, as it can be wheeled around the house and will provide a better quality of life. It is boring for a parrot to spend its whole life in the same room. Some cages have a top opening. This is not particularly useful because if you let your parrot out from the top it will be encouraged to spend a lot of time on the top of the cage (and perhaps nibble the walls!). Also, you will want to teach your parrot to step onto your hand in order to come out, and this is difficult if you have to reach down into the cage. However, cages with a top opening are easier to clean thoroughly.

Most cages come with a grid above the removable tray. Parrots like to play on the cage floor, so it is best to remove the grid and use it only when you remove the tray. I prefer to use

Left: *This cage is not spacious enough for two birds. It is also the wrong shape and should be wider than it is tall.*

newspaper on the cage floor except with white cockatoos. If they play around with the paper they will soon have gray breasts. Some parrots shred the newspaper; this is not a problem and it gives them something to do. The alternatives are sand and wood shavings, which make a mess, or the more expensive woodchip products for animal use. Cage trays need to be cleaned daily, so newspaper is a cheap and quick solution.

Minimum cage sizes

Only a few countries have legislation defining minimum cage sizes for parrots. With the increase in animal welfare concerns, it is likely that such legislation will become more widespread in the future. In the United States, a parrot measuring more than 30 inches (75 cm) in length (for example, a Blue and Yellow Macaw) must be kept in a cage 3 feet x 2 feet x 5 feet (90 cm x 60 cm x 150 cm). This means that pet stores will not sell large macaws—and this is in the interest of these birds because it prevents impulse buying. It is therefore advisable to buy a large cage at the outset.

Cage cover

Whether you need to buy a cage cover will depend on the circumstances. If you have a parrot that is noisy early in the morning, or if the cage is located where car headlights or security lights could cause problems, a cover is a good idea. Be sure to wash it regularly because it will attract feather dust.

Above: *Horizontal cage bars make climbing easier for the parrot.*

PERCHES

Be prepared to change at least one of the perches in a new cage because they will probably all be of the same thickness. Parrots need to alter their grip and many will prefer thin perches. A large cage that I bought for an Amazon contained perches 1⅛ inches (2.7 cm) thick. When I cut a thin apple-wood branch for the cage, the Amazon used it immediately. Note that cheap cages usually come with plastic perches—an unhealthy surface for the feet. Parrot owners need access to apple trees so that they can cut fresh perches at regular intervals.

FOOD CONTAINERS

Before you buy a cage, examine the food and water containers. You must be able to remove these from outside the cage. Even the tamest parrot can object to hands placed inside except for the purpose of taking him out. How many containers are there? There should be one for water and preferably two or three others. If there are only two, buy one or two more of the type shown opposite that can screw onto the bars of the cage.

Stainless steel coop cups are very popular. I use them extensively as they are so easy to keep clean. The main disadvantages are that some parrots can remove the cups from the rings. There is no answer to this except to use a different kind of container, but

Left: *A branch made from apple wood makes an excellent perch.*

Left: *Stainless steel container that screws onto the cage bars.*
Right: *A plastic gravity container can be used to provide drinking water for small parrots.*

note that some parrots can unhook those that are not screwed on. If a duplicate set of cups is obtained, it reduces feeding time or at least allows the cups to be washed later, so that offering fresh food takes priority.

For really mischievous and destructive parrots, the containers mentioned will be useless. Swing feeders are essential for two reasons. One is that most types are designed with a retaining bar that makes it impossible for the dishes to be removed, and the other is for personal safety. It is no fun having an aggressive parrot trying to take a chunk out of your hand at feeding time! The dishes are built into a frame that swings around, blocking the exit and allowing the dishes to be changed with ease.

Plastic gravity-type containers are designed to hold several days' supply of seed for one small bird, such as a Budgerigar, but if the seed in the lip becomes wet or soiled it can hold up the flow of seed. The containers can also be used for water, but as a backup supply or drinking water only, as most birds need a large dish of water in which to bathe. While some people might suggest that they would be useful if someone had to leave a bird for a weekend. I believe that birds should never be left unattended overnight. The other problem with this type of feeder is that there are too many corners so they are not easy to keep clean. A small brush must be used.

Make sure that the cage is kept clean and that food and water containers are thoroughly washed daily. Failure to do this will result in your parrot being exposed to harmful bacteria. Dark-colored plastic cups conceal the accumulation of dirt, so take a piece of paper towel and dig into the corners. You might be surprised how much dirt is there.

STANDS

A stand or play stand is a perch away from its cage where a parrot can sit when supervised. There are some well-designed models that incorporate perches, feeders, ladders, a pullout tray, and an apron to contain seed and droppings. These go under the name of "recreation centers." When toys and ropes are added, this is exactly what they are.

A stand does not need to be expensive. If you're buying a new cage, you might think twice about also purchasing a stand. You can make one at a small cost using a large flower pot as a mold for the base. Fill it with cement. Before the cement dries, make a hole in the center for a branch. Searching for a branch with a right angle is worth the effort. Another inexpensive alternative is to buy a second-hand coffee table and make a hole in the middle to take a branch or a T-shaped perch. It is extremely important that parrots have a regular perch away from their cage. In this way they can easily be placed in various rooms in the house, to make life more interesting. To be permanently surrounded by bars is not healthy for their state of mind.

Some full-winged parrots might be reluctant to use a stand, so it must be made attractive with favored food items in the container, fresh-cut twigs to gnaw on, and a favorite toy. A parrot that does not use a stand will perch in unsuitable places; eventually this might lead to the bird being confined to its cage. Tops of doors are taboo because of the danger of injury (or even death if the door suddenly slams shut) and the likelihood of damage to the door. Furniture will also be damaged. Curtain rods should be out of bounds because of the difficulty of retrieving a parrot from a high place.

Left: *An inexpensive stand can be made using a large flower pot filled with concrete for the base.*

TOYS

An enormous range of parrot toys is available in large pet stores or from mail-order companies. I would recommend toys made from natural materials such as wood, leather, and rope. Some companies produce species-specific toys developed through research — but remember that individual preference can never be predicted. Toys are important in introducing parrots to unusual shapes and textures, and to encourage natural inquisitiveness and foraging behavior.

When choosing metal toys or ones with metal hangers, look at the labels; choose stainless steel, and avoid any that contain zinc (see Chapter 8). Plastic toys are not suitable for a macaw or any species with a strong beak. Inspect a toy carefully before buying it. Obviously, there should be no open links or sharp surfaces. Most parrots seem to prefer natural materials and colors, although a friend's Amazon has a purple child's toy that she adores! Brightly colored acrylic toys might look trendy and eye-catching, but many parrots avoid them. Money can be saved by buying children's toys from garage sales and thrift stores. Wash and sterilize them before use.

For highly intelligent species, you can buy puzzles; a parrot might have to undo several links to remove the nut inside it. Such toys can be recommended because they amuse a parrot for a long period. Swings and rope ladders are excellent because they encourage activity. Young birds of almost any parrot species will soon learn to use a swing, if presented with one at the weaning stage. An older parrot that has never been offered toys might disdain them or take years to show an interest. In that case, initially buy only a couple of wooden toys and keep up a supply of fresh-cut branches for gnawing. You should rotate toys — leave them in the cage for two or three weeks and then change them for others.

Above left: *Parrots love to experiment with a variety of textured objects, but some will avoid brightly colored toys such as these.*

Above right: *Choose stainless steel toys and avoid any that may contain zinc.*

For many parrots the most enjoyable games are not those with expensive toys, but merely being on a table for the fun of throwing spoons, bottle caps, small cardboard boxes, or pieces of uncooked pasta onto the floor. Parrots never tire of watching these hit the ground!

BOX OR SLEEPING TENT

Some small parrot species, notably conures, caiques, and lorikeets, like to roost in holes. They will feel much more secure if they can retire to a box or a sleeping tent (available from some pet stores). A small cardboard box with a hole cut in it will suffice for a while, but will eventually be destroyed.

BUYING A YOUNG PARROT

If you buy from a breeder you might be able to choose from several young parrots (nest mates) and you can ask for a hatch certificate (it shows the date of hatching). The age of the parrots will depend on the species. For example, you would buy an Amazon or a Gray Parrot at about 14 weeks, but a cockatoo or macaw would not be weaned until about 5 or 6 months or later, depending on the species. If you buy from another source and you have little experience with parrots, how can you be sure that you are buying a young bird?

Above: *Pieces of dry pasta can be used as toys.*
Left: *An adult Gray parrot can be distinguished by its yellow eyes.*

Unscrupulous sellers almost invariably describe an older bird as "6 months old" because most people would not consider buying a parrot after this age.

Fortunately, there are differences, subtle or otherwise, between young and adult parrots. All very young ones have an appealing, vulnerable appearance that results from the dark eyes, lighter bare facial skin, and soft-looking plumage, and their rhythmic head-bobbing action to solicit food. In long-tailed species the tail is shorter.

Except in species where adults have brown eyes, the eye color is the first clue. For example, in Gray Parrots the eye color changes slowly from gray to yellow over a period of about 18 months;

in Amazons with orange eyes, such as the Blue-front, the gray-brown eye becomes dull orange by the age of about 5 months; in Blue and Yellow and in Green-winged Macaws the grayish eyes of recently fledged young turn pale yellow by about 18 months. In the Green-winged Macaw the lower mandible is partly light-colored in birds under about 6 months old. In Hahn's Macaw the gray-brown iris becomes reddish brown by the age of about 5 months.

In *Pionus* such as the Blue-headed the eyes are dark brown, but young can be distinguished by their duller plumage. Some birds have the frontal band red or another color not found in the adult.

In some parrot species the distinct markings of

Left: *Young Gray Parrots have dark eyes.*

adults are poorly defined. For example, in the Senegal Parrot the plumage is much duller until the first molt at about 1 year. In the Jardine's Parrot the head is dusky brown and the wing markings are only hinted at. In very young birds the cere is pink and the base of the upper mandible is light. The iris is gray, changing to red-brown at 12 to 18 months, whereas in the Senegal the eye color changes from dark gray to light gray to yellow over a period of about 18 months. In very young birds, the beak is pink at the base of the upper mandible.

Small parrots usually mature more quickly. Young lovebirds have a dark tip to their beak and paler plumage. Adult appearance is attained at 5 months. *Pyrrhura* conures, such as the Green-cheeked, are almost indistinguishable from adults at that age.

HOW TO FIND A PARROT

In North America, parrots are usually purchased from a pet store. It is usually best to buy a parrot from a breeder, but many breeders follow the unfortunate practice of selling young before they are weaned. Only experienced hand-rearers should buy unweaned young. The huge disadvantage of store-bought parrots is that it is unlikely that all the birds have been bought from one source. When young reared in different localities come together they are susceptible to diseases, especially viral diseases. Their immune systems are not yet fully functional and if they encounter a disease agent that was not present in their previous locality, such as PBFD (see Chapter 8), they will have no resistance. Because Budgerigars and Cockatiels often carry psittacosis (chlamydiosis), young parrots housed in the same premises often pick up the disease, possibly with fatal consequences. Another risky situation is where captive-bred parrots are sold on the same premises as wild-caught parrots, with a risk of the former contracting some disease from the latter.

To find a breeder, contact a local or national parrot club, search the Internet, or look in an aviculture or parrot magazine. Give preference to a breeder who asks you a few questions to determine your suitability as the custodian of one

of his or her parrots, rather than one who concentrates on informing you of the price. If you are purchasing a wild-caught bird, be sure to ask if the parrot offered to you is closed-ringed and captive-bred. Remember that many wild-caught parrots that have passed through quarantine are ringed (banded), but if you look closely you will see that the ring is not fully closed.

The purchaser of a young parrot might fail to notice important aspects of how it has been kept and fed. Some parrots are very nervous when moved to a new location, so the purchaser should note the location and type of food containers in the cage. If, for example, a young parrot has been feeding from a low perch with food containers at the same level, and it is

Above: *You might seek out a breeder with an aviary in order to buy a young parrot.*

placed in a larger cage, the bird will probably climb to the higher perch, but might be very reluctant to climb down to feed. Therefore, it is a good idea to buy some hook-on feeders in case the parrot needs to feed at perch level until it has settled in.

Buying a cage and toys is only the first part of the process. Understanding what to do with them is also important. I recall an occasion when someone came to my home and asked me to take a male Cockatiel. I did not hesitate to say yes; she kept him in a bedroom because her dog continually jumped up at his cage. The Cockatiel appeared to be no older than about 1 year and had been bought from a pet store four months previously. He was in good condition but seemed ill at ease in the cage. I had no trouble in placing Joey in a spacious aviary where he joined about 14 others of his own species. An untamed bird of a flock species, like the Cockatiel, should not be condemned to a lonely life.

I recall a comment once made on a television program by an employee of a pet rescue center. He said that all birds brought in are re-homed in aviaries. He missed the point. A tame bird used to human companionship is likely to be just as unhappy in an aviary as that untamed Cockatiel was in a cage on his own.

The moment I set eyes on Joey's cage I knew that his owner understood little about making a caged bird happy. The cage was much too small, suitable only for a Budgerigar. There was

Below: *Joey's cage, as shown below, was too small and filled with unsuitable objects.*

a perch at one end at the top, the other end being occupied by a large swing that the Cockatiel never used. This meant it could not jump from perch to perch. The cage contained a ladder, toys, mirror, and a large piece of cuttlefish bone. There was not a lot of room for the Cockatiel to move around and he often clung to the bars. Food and water containers were not an integral part of the cage so hands entered it to replenish them. The water container was a violent purple plastic hook-on, the sort of color that a sensitive bird owner would not purchase. A millet spray was hanging in front of a gravity feeder, obscuring the contents, which was inconsequential; it was obvious the contents would not be touched by a Cockatiel. It was a parakeet mixture that contained colorful small pellets. As the pellets were heavier than the small seeds, they dropped into the accessible part of the feeder, obscuring the small seeds that the Cockatiel would have eaten if he was adventurous enough to throw out the pellets. Another food container held panicum millet, and this, together with the millet spray, was his sole diet.

It occurred to me that there must be thousands of parrots living in small cages like this one, furnished with alien objects made of plastic or acrylic (toys) and shiny objects (mirrors) that are of no interest to them and just get in their way. Tame birds, on the other hand, love their toys (see page 65).

The biggest improvement to Joey's life, short of the aviary in which he now resides, would have been a large cage in which he could stretch his wings. It would contain twiggy apple branches, with fresh bark to nibble on, not smooth plastic perches. The cage design would include food and water containers and a pull-out tray on the floor to prevent the intrusive action of a hand entering the cage. All too often, an inexpensive cage is purchased for an inexpensive bird. This usually has a plastic base that clips onto the cage, not a pull-out tray, which is suitable for a tame bird, but not for one that panics when a hand enters the cage.

Above: *A toy should not be too large for the size of the cage.*

TAKING AN UNWANTED PARROT

I admire those who say: "If I buy a hand-reared young parrot I am encouraging breeders to produce more, which is wrong when there are so many parrots that need a good home." However, to rehome a parrot needs a certain level of experience, especially if it has been neglected or treated badly. Sometimes, due to circumstances, parrots are given away and they end up in the hands of inexperienced people. This results in problems and then the unfortunate parrot is either moved yet again or its owner, cruelly inconsiderate of the bird's psychological requirements, might enclose it in a room on its own.

You may have always wanted a parrot, for example, but might not have been able afford to buy one and a big cage. Then a friend offers you an Orange-winged Amazon that he acquired recently. You don't ask why he no longer wants it and jump at the opportunity, not realizing that not all parrots are suitable as pets. Wild-caught birds in particular can never be tamed, are very afraid of people, and scream when anyone approaches their cage. Close confinement is torture for them. If the parrot is an adult (the eye is orange) it should be placed in an aviary with another Amazon. If it is young (the eye is brown) it may become tame with caring and patient people

who can spend a lot of time with it—always assuming that it survives for more than a few weeks.

Before agreeing to take on a parrot, go and see it. Observe how it reacts to you. It could show immediate fear or dislike, in which case do not consider taking it. Do not get too close to the cage (unless it is very tame), speak quietly, and keep your arms by your side! Inexperienced people can be much too pushy in their behavior, sticking their hand in the cage and expecting the parrot to "Step up" (see page 122) or making inappropriate movements that put the bird on its guard. The result is a bite that leaves them thinking the parrot is unreliable, and not for them, when it was not the parrot whose behavior was wrong. Go out of the room, leaving the bird alone, and see if it screams and how loud it is.

Opposite: *Cockatiels are hand-reared for pets.*
Right: *Parrots in the wild are never alone. They are highly social creatures.*

Accept that parrots are not like dogs that fawn over anyone who pays them attention. They are individuals who know their own minds and who often make snap judgments about people that are difficult to reverse. They might dislike someone because of the color of their hair or because of a beard that is unfamiliar to them, or they might prefer members of the opposite sex. So before you go to see the parrot, keep an open mind. Don't acquire it just because you have already made up your mind to do so. Do not be afraid to tell the owner that you need to think about it. Your parrot should be your companion for life, so this partnership requires careful thought.

Be aware that a parrot that is being sold at a low price or given away might have severe

behavioral problems as a result of being in unsympathetic hands. It might be a wild-caught bird that has proved impossible to tame and is not suitable as a companion bird—only for an aviary. If it has never been tamed or it has been mistreated, it could be one to two years before it starts to respond to you. Most people give up long before this stage is reached; they have neither the time nor the patience to deal with such a parrot. They might have taken it because it was cheap or free, with little or no understanding of the difficulties involved in rehabilitating it emotionally. In unsympathetic hands its behavior will worsen—until it is given away yet again.

JOINING A PARROT CLUB

Parrot clubs exist in many areas where parrots are popular companions. Most clubs tend to focus on pets, but the emphasis might equally be on breeding. To discover if there is a parrot club in your area, contact a local breeder or buy a parrot or aviculture magazine. Joining such a club is beneficial, not only for the advice given by speakers, but because you can probably find out where to locate a breeder of a certain species and, more importantly, an avian vet (a vet who treats parrots). You can also make friends with like-minded people and learn from their experiences.

Left: *These three tame Gray Parrots are placed in an aviary during the day when the weather is good. Playing together, climbing, and foraging enriches their lives.*

4

Your parrot as a family member

Parrots are categorized as pets, along with dogs, cats, and guinea pigs, yet many have the potential to be a companion whose presence is almost as satisfying as that of a human. (Some would say more so!) This is the result of their intelligence, social awareness, and ability to mimic. Of these qualities the latter is the least important. The other two qualities, intelligence and social awareness, make them extraordinary companions that deserve a great deal of respect and attention.

When you acquire a parrot, try to fathom out what it is thinking, how it sees the world, and what it needs to keep it happy. The unending heartbreaking stories of parrots that have sat in a cage for years, with no physical contact and little attention, cause me to emphasize the psychological and emotional needs of parrots: they are as strong and as real as those of a human. If you do not have time to treat your parrot like a family member, to give it love, and to do everything possible to make its life happy, please do not buy one.

Opposite: *This Ringneck Parakeet is truly a member of the family.*

Before you bring a parrot into your home, check the rooms it will occupy and try to assess potential hazards. Could it fall behind a piece of furniture where you could not retrieve the bird without dismantling the furniture? Could it disappear into a space behind the fireplace?

Check for other possible danger areas. When your parrot arrives you must introduce it to windows. You might forget that a young parrot does not understand the existence of glass. It needs to know that window frames hold a hard, clear substance. If your bird can be handled readily, take it to a window and move forward until its beak gently touches the pane. Do this a couple of times a day in different locations. If it is full-winged, let it out of the cage only when the curtains are closed until it has learned this lesson.

LOCATION OF THE CAGE

Your parrot should reside in the most lived-in room in the house, unless it is the kitchen. Do not place your parrot's cage near an electrical field; that is, keep it away from computers, televisions, and microwave ovens. They can have an adverse effect on its health. Avoid locations that are in direct sunlight. A corner of the room, or against one wall is usually the best place, because this offers a feeling of security. Above all, if there are smokers in the family, absolutely forbid them to smoke on the same floor. Secondary smoke is extremely harmful to birds and can cause their death.

Left: *A parrot must be discouraged from perching on hazardous places like a door.*
Opposite: *Macaws, like all parrots, are extremely observant birds.*

COMMUNICATE INFORMATION

Treat your parrot like a family member by imparting useful information in an intelligent way. All parrots, even the smallest species, who live in close contact with people understand a lot more than we realize, partly because birds are intensely observant. This fact means that we can give them a lot of information. We already do so subconsciously; for example, putting on your coat, or picking up your keys and saying "Bye-bye" imparts the fact that you are going out. With a little thought, however, you can tell them how long you will be gone. In my house I have two Amazons and an Iris Lorikeet. If I am going out to pick some seeding dock or some hawthorn berries, or if I am going to the post office, I show them the letters or parcels before I say: "Bye-bye. Back in a minute." If I am going shopping, which means an absence of about three hours, I tell

them: "Bye-bye. See you later!" and make sure that they see my shopping bag. During these absences the radio is always switched on to a music station, for the parrots' entertainment.

Many of our comings and goings are routine, so our birds know when to expect our return (and they do have a very precise sense of time). They will also anticipate the arrival of their favorite person when they hear his or her car. If I plan to be absent for several hours longer than normal, I partly draw down the roller blind on the window nearest my Amazon's cage. This arose out of the practical need to protect her from the late afternoon sun, as nothing distresses her more than being in direct sunlight. It also alerts her to the fact that I will be gone for a few hours.

The senses of parrots are more finely tuned than ours. Their sight is better (they can see birds of prey high in the sky that are invisible to us), and they hear better (they were used during World War II to warn of incoming aircraft). I have no proof of their sense of smell, but Irene Christie, a well-known parrot advisor in the United Kingdom, tells me that in her macaw Max, who starred in the James Bond film *For Your Eyes Only*, this is well developed. If she is cooking something he likes, even though he cannot see it, he will yell until he gets some. She sometimes goes to homes where other parrots live. On her return he becomes agitated and nips at her neck, and Irene is convinced that he can smell the other parrots.

DAILY SCHEDULE

A mistake often made during the first couple of months after purchase is to give a parrot more time and attention than will be possible on a permanent basis. As the novelty of this appealing young creature wears off, so is the time devoted to it reduced. This is a recipe for a noisy, demanding parrot. It craves attention but is not getting enough, thus behavioral problems set in. In my opinion, a set daily schedule is a good idea. The parrot soon learns that at certain times of the day it cannot receive so much attention. It is not forever expectantly bouncing up and down by the door!

Maintaining a contented parrot is very much a matter of giving it a certain amount of focused attention, or "quality time," plus a lot of peripheral attention on a daily basis. I would suggest set daily periods of perhaps 60 minutes with you,

Left: *A table-top stand can easily be moved around the house.*

Opposite: *Fresh-cut branches will keep your parrots amused for hours.*

or 30 minutes twice daily, when you can devote your full attention to the parrot. If you quickly establish a routine it will feel more secure. If it has no idea when it will get your attention, it will scream. At other times maintain vocal contact by speaking to it as often as possible, even if only briefly, whenever you pass its cage, and give it tidbits or items to chew. Place the bird on its play stand under the (hopefully) watchful eye of another family member, but do not leave it unattended. Make sure it has interesting items on its stand because, if the parrot is full-winged, it will not stay long if there is nothing to do there.

As well as the obvious aids to keeping a parrot occupied, such as a fresh-cut apple branch or even a rolled-up newspaper pushed through the cage bars, you can teach your parrot simple tricks, or how to whistle a tune, or sing to it (if it's an Amazon).

At all times you must consider what is best for your parrot. It needs a lot of sleep when young, at least 10 hours at night. If it does not get sufficient sleep it will be irritable, which might result in nipping, and it might not feed well. All parrots need a quiet rest period during the afternoon. Do not take the parrot out for a play period during the early afternoon as it will be naturally sleepy then. A common mistake of the inexperienced owner is to let the parrot spend hours outside its cage, and to allow it to feed at the table. A young parrot needs to eat frequently; it should not be away from its cage for more than about one hour at a time. Allowing it to eat at the table might set a pattern that could result in its refusing to eat in its cage. Just imagine the consequences if you need to go away and the temporary caregiver cannot let it out!

ENVIRONMENTAL ENRICHMENT

Environmental enrichment is normally used in the context of animals and birds in outdoor enclosures, but it applies equally to parrots in the home.

Although you could improve a parrot's quality of life by giving it access to an outdoor aviary, you may not be in a position to do this. A small spare room, on the other hand, that is not in use has many of the benefits of an outdoor aviary and none of the disadvantages. All the room needs is screens secured over the windows, carpets and furniture removed, and branches installed for perching. Ropes and swings can be hung

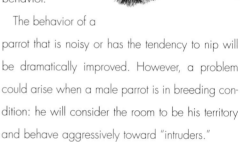

from the ceiling and cardboard boxes and logs strewn around the floor for destruction. Bunches of seeding grass or branches bearing blossoms or berries encourage natural foraging behavior.

The behavior of a parrot that is noisy or has the tendency to nip will be dramatically improved. However, a problem could arise when a male parrot is in breeding condition: he will consider the room to be his territory and behave aggressively toward "intruders."

From an early age, take your parrot with you in a small pet carrier when you visit friends. Some parrots love a trip in the car and become excited as soon as they see the carrier; broadening their horizons in this way is the best method of producing a well-socialized parrot that is not likely to become distrustful or easily stressed.

Left: *Branches with berries (or blossoms) encourage natural foraging behavior.*
Above: *Parrots can entertain themselves for hours with ropes and swings.*

SECURITY IN THE HOME

Theft of parrots is common. Macaws, cockatoos, and Gray Parrots are most likely to catch the eye of a thief, but all species are vulnerable. Do not advertise the presence of your bird by placing its cage in a window that looks onto the street. If the cage is visible from the street, use blinds to reduce visibility. Never leave a door or window unlocked when you leave the premises and, most important, install a burglar alarm. If your house was broken into your insurance company would replace your valuables, but nothing and nobody can replace your parrot. Protect your parrot from the stress that it would endure when snatched away from everything it knows and the almost certain rough handling it would encounter.

Your parrot should be microchipped. Most parrots can be identified unequivocally only by the number on the chip. If stolen and recovered by police, this may be the only acceptable method of identification, as rings can be removed. Microchipping is not 100 percent foolproof because, on rare occasions, the microchip cannot be found when the bird is scanned, but this is rare. Each microchip bears a unique number and can be implanted quickly and safely into the breast of even small parrots. (Microchipping into the leg is not recommended because it can cause lameness.) Note that some companies that carry out blood tests for sexing and disease diagnosis will store DNA from blood samples on request. Matching a blood sample from your bird (if it is recovered) with the sample stored is another way of proving ownership.

Right: *A microchip can be implanted into the bird's breast.*

FREEDOM INSIDE AND OUTSIDE THE ROOM

A parrot that does not use a stand will perch in unsuitable places; eventually this might lead to its being confined to its cage. Tops of doors are taboo because of the danger of injury and the likelihood of damage to the door. Furniture will also be damaged. Curtain rods should be out of bounds because of the difficulty of retrieving a parrot from a high place and the strong possibility it will chew up the drapes.

Free flight outside the house is an idea that finds favor with a few people. Even the tamest and most sensible parrot can take off suddenly if it receives a sudden fright and might fly so far in panic that it cannot find its way home. If you have a large property with some trees and no close neighbors, you might succeed for a while to fly your parrot at liberty, but the chances are that eventually you will lose it forever. Never try this with nomadic species like Budgerigars and Cockatiels. They have no homing instinct.

One lady regularly took her two Gray Parrots to the park with her dogs, and allowed them to fly free. Then the inevitable happened. One of them flew off, never to be seen again. I feel sad for both the Grays, but I have no sympathy for the owner. Allowing them liberty in these circumstances can only be described as negligent. Even if they are carefully trained, the risk is high.

Contrast this with a very exciting project in Washington State, where a group of parrot lovers rented an unused barn and met twice a week to allow their parrots to fly. They were the thinking ones! The quality of their birds' lives was improved beyond measure. About 25 people brought a wide variety of parrots that, before they joined the group, were examined by a vet to reduce the disease transmission risk. Mona Delgado wrote: "Everyone agrees that the most fun at the building is when different species of parrots take off in a flock and fly about over our heads for extended periods of time. This is breathtaking. Many of the birds take off in pairs and threesomes, fly as a group, and even change direction together. The more time the birds spend in the air, the stronger they get, and the longer their later flyabouts become." (To start with, many of these parrots had little or no confidence in their ability to take off, to avoid obstacles, and to land.) Obviously this kind of exercise had important implications for the chances of retrieving them if they escaped because they were trained to fly back to the owner and had the confidence to fly down.

Preventing an escape

The majority of escaped parrots are never found, so take these steps to prevent escape:

- Do not allow a small parrot to sit on your shoulder. It is too easy to walk outside, forgetting it is there. Do not be lulled into a false sense of security because your parrot never leaves you in the house. If it is frightened it will take off. Instinct tells it to flee.

- If your parrot is wing-clipped, check its flight feathers every 10 to 14 days. A parrot is able to fly with only three full-length primaries in each wing.

- Impress on family members that doors and windows must be kept closed when the parrot is out, or do not let it out when family members who cannot observe this rule are present. In summertime, if necessary, have a screen door made, or use a "curtain" made of aluminum chains over the door. Lock the outer doors so that no one can enter unexpectedly when the bird is out.

- Be aware that harnesses are not necessarily safe. Some parrots are clever enough to undo them.

Finding an escapee

Here is what you can do in the event that your bird escapes:

- Telephone the local radio station with a description of the escapee.
- Send a story to local papers and include a photograph of a bird of the same species.
- Place notices in local shops and pet stores.
- Make some flyers on your computer and place them on your gate and other prominent places.
- Inform the police.
- Inform local animal rescue centers.
- Contact a local birdwatching group. Members are more likely than the average person to spot an unusual bird.
- Inform your local branch of a pet-watch organization, if there is one.
- Inform the secretary of the local cage-bird society or nearest parrot club.
- Report the loss to a local veterinarian in case the bird has been taken there—perhaps found injured.
- Keep careful note of the ring number and microchip of your bird. In the event of someone finding it and not wishing to part with it, these numbers might be the only proof of your ownership.

FINDING YOUR PARROT

When a parrot escapes, the chances of locating it can be greatly increased if quick action is taken. The exceptions are Cockatiels and small lorikeets, which are nomadic and skillful flyers even if they have been caged for years, and macaws. Most parrots do not go far unless the escape was triggered by fear. If a parrot was taken (unwisely) into the yard and was frightened away by a sudden event, it might fly a long way and become lost and disorientated.

If your publicity campaign brings a flurry of telephone calls, do not be too optimistic. Ask questions, because members of the public are not good at noticing details—only the bright colors. If you locate your bird, take an empty cage to the area and, if it had one, its bell, which you can ring. If you have one, also take the most vocal parrot you own, in a securely locked cage. Your parrot might be too frightened of flying down to

Below: *Every parrotkeeper should own a bird net with a padded rim.*

come to you. If he is not tame, avoid any action that will frighten him away, such as placing a tall ladder in the tree. You need patience, an empty cage baited with favorite food items, and a long line attached to the door in such a way that once the bird enters a quick tug will close the door. You must wait patiently until the parrot enters the cage. Don't be hasty, because if you pull the line too soon and the parrot flies off, he will be too suspicious to return.

ARE HARNESSES SAFE?

Parrot harnesses were developed in the United States, where they are widely used. A harness fits around the parrot's body, similar to a dog harness. However, unlike some dogs, most parrots object to the feeling of something enclosing them. It seems wrong to try to restrain a parrot as though it is a mammal.

Cockatoos and macaws probably tolerate this better than smaller species. Some parrots accept a harness only after months of perseverance by the owner, but such persistence causes stress. It can also cause the parrot to pluck itself. Safety is another issue. Some parrots can work out how to undo a harness—with potentially disastrous results. Carelessness when using a harness, because the owner has not held it securely, has resulted in many parrots flying off. Parrots can also bite through one. However, in some cases a harness has improved a parrot's quality of life because the bird is able to go out of the house, even if it is only taken to the car for a journey.

Below: *Wearing a harness is a stressful experience for many parrots. Two hours after wearing one for the first time, this young Gray Parrot started to pluck its feathers.*

KEEPING MORE THAN ONE PARROT

People have differing views on keeping more than one companion parrot in the home. They need to take into account the varying circumstances. If a parrot has been the sole bird in the house for many years and is closely bonded to its owner, the arrival of another is certain to cause jealousy and rivalry. On the other hand a young parrot, only a few months in its home, might welcome another parrot, whether or not it was the same species. The same would probably apply to an older parrot that did not have a close bond with any family member or one that had never been tamed. Parrots are extremely social birds

and, lacking a close relationship with a human, they might make friends with another parrot regardless of the discrepancy in size.

Carol, a single-bird owner, looked after her friend's Black-headed Caique while she was on vacation. Carol's macaw has a very close relationship with her, so Carol was uncertain how the macaw would react. In fact, he did not seem to mind at all and every day he would wish the caique "Good morning!" However, instead of using his normal tone of voice, he spoke in a higher-pitched tone, as a human would use for a baby!

Some cockatoos seem to crave a relationship with their own species. It is possible that if a second cockatoo is acquired, the original one will bond to it so quickly and so strongly that its human companion will be totally ignored. Wild-caught parrots, trapped as adults, desperately need the companionship of their own kind. This might be the only way to give some quality of life to a parrot that remembers the wild.

The main factor to consider before acquiring a second parrot is that the two birds might never be friends and, worse still, might maintain a hatred for each other. According to an article in *Parrots* magazine, "… there is a chance they will never get on. Given parrots' long lifespans, we are talking about years of animosity, separate cages, separate time out of the cages, and double the work. I have met many owners who have incompatible birds and have to keep them permanently in different areas of the house, so strong is the hostility between them."

Some parrot owners naively believe they can bring a second parrot home and keep it in the same cage. This shows a lack of understanding

Opposite: *A male and female Eclectus kept together need an aviary.*

Above right: *If you own a macaw and acquire a second one, they might never be friends.*

of the territorial nature of a parrot. Its cage is its territory and intruders will be attacked! There are always exceptions, but to experiment is to take a risk that could result in one parrot losing its life or being injured. Only when two young birds are acquired and placed in the cage at the same time can you expect them to cohabit happily—at least for a while.

Jealousy can be an overpowering emotion in parrots. It is most likely to occur in one that has enjoyed a close relationship with its owner for some years. When a second parrot arrives its behavior can change dramatically for the worse. One can liken it to an only child who, at the age of 10 years or so, greets the arrival of a baby brother or sister with abhorrence and loathing. The older child is no longer the center of attention and the household becomes a place of turmoil.

These days there is often a very different scenario to the conventional single companion parrot in the home. Some parrot lovers have as many as a dozen because they take on unwanted birds. This could be a recipe for disaster, but Angela Furniss, who runs a parrot club in the United Kingdom, has found a good solution to the problem of housing a number of parrots in an average-sized (or smaller than average) home. She built an outdoor aviary that measures 12 x 20 feet (3.6 x 6 m). During the day (weather permitting) each member of her varied group of parrots is taken to the aviary. There friendships soon form and when the parrots are brought back indoors at night they share a cage with a friend. For example, a Blue-fronted Amazon, aged at least 36, usually sleeps with a Gray Parrot, but sometimes he goes into the cage of a young Military Macaw. A Timneh Gray and a caique live together, as do a Senegal Parrot and a conure. In this unconventional pet situation each parrot chooses its companion.

Right: *Giardia is a problem in the Cockatiel, resulting in feather plucking.*
Opposite: *Spraying with a mister keeps the plumage of this Yellow-fronted Amazon in good condition.*

CORRECT HUMIDITY

When keeping more than one parrot in the same room, consider that species from different environments require different degrees of humidity. Birds from rain forests, such as Grays, macaws, and Amazons, need higher humidity to keep their plumage and skin in good condition. A dry environment could cause dry plumage, feather

plucking, and erratic behavior. They should not be kept close to the dry heat of a radiator. On the other hand, if you have a species from a near-desert or desert environment, such as the Cockatiel, high humidity could cause skin problems and even feather plucking and fungal diseases. Frequent spraying (at least every other day), bathing, or showering usually counteracts the dry environment of a centrally heated or air-conditioned room. Note that a parrot fed on pellets or extruded foods needs constant access to water, as these absorb moisture from the body. Spraying and bathing lubricates the skin of the feet as well as benefiting the feathers. Therefore, if you decide to acquire a second parrot, do some reading on the environment from which the two species originate to ensure that they will be compatible.

HEALTH RISK TO YOU

It is important to keep your parrot's cage and environment in a clean and hygienic condition and to try to remove as much feather dust from the air as possible (see Chapter 8). This is important for your health and that of your family. Humans can suffer from a condition known as birdkeeper's lung, or hypersensitive pneumonitis. It is rarely diagnosed correctly because doctors mistake it for asthma. Medication can halt the condition, which apparently can result in pulmonary fibrosis.

OTHER PETS

Whether a relationship between a parrot and another pet can be successful is unpredictable. It would usually be asking for trouble to introduce a small parrot into a household containing cats, although if a kitten grows up with a larger parrot it will probably learn a degree of respect for that sharp beak! Be aware that a parrot or a cockatoo has the strength to kill or maim a dog. Some parrots, such as Grays and Amazons, delight in teasing animals, tweaking their tails, and flying off. They can make the animal's life a misery, so train a parrot from an early age not to do this. Also train a puppy not to touch parrots. Fearless little caiques are notorious for interacting with other animals. They might befriend an animal, bite it, or continually harass it.

If you have animals and parrots in the house do not become complacent about their relationships. This could change in an instant and result in the death of one. Think carefully about letting a friend with an animal care for your parrot in their home while you are on vacation. Some people are unaware of the dangers other pets pose to parrots.

Below: *Always supervise any contact between a household dog and your parrot; their behavior can be unpredictable when interacting with each other.*

TRAVELING WITH YOUR PARROT

It has already been mentioned that you should buy a traveling box even before you buy your parrot. The plastic carriers made for dogs are suitable, or you can buy a special bird carrier made from lightweight clear plastic, containing a perch, feeders, and toy hanger. Another type is a small cage that fits into a specially designed backpack with padded shoulder straps. For a large parrot, such as a macaw, you will need to buy the strongest dog carrier available.

You should train your parrot to enter and travel in the carrier from a very early age. Put a treat inside every day and leave the parrot there for five minutes, or walk around the yard carrying the bird in the carrier. It will then look forward to going inside. No matter how tame your parrot is,

it is asking for trouble to carry it out to the car on your hand or shoulder.

Parrots that are used to going in a car travel well by this method, and often enjoy it very much. Obviously the parrot must never be left alone in the car under any circumstances. This would be tempting thieves; also, high temperatures could cause its death. If you must move a nervous parrot to a new location, especially when driving at night, cover the front of the box with a towel. Nervous parrots travel best in a small, dark place, such as a wooden box.

If you must take your parrot on an airplane, remember that the box must conform to IATA (International Air Transport Association) and any other local specifications, so check with the airline to ensure that your container is suitable. You can only travel with an airline that has a license to carry livestock, so check with the company before you book the flight. Only in rare circumstances will a parrot be allowed to enter the cabin. Normally it will travel in a heated cargo hold.

Left: *A pet carrier for larger parrots must have a door made of stainless steel—not plastic.*

5

Behavior: how to avoid problems

Many behavioral problems result from mismanagement during the weaning period and soon after, especially if the parrot was force-weaned or had its wings clipped at a very early age. Such mistakes almost guarantee a problem-filled first few months. Sudden neglect after weaning also creates problems. One example was a young Gray Parrot that was sold to a nursery. Imagine being a hand-reared parrot that had been the focus of human attention right up to the day it was sold, then being placed in an aviary and ignored. About four weeks later a kind-hearted lady bought it, not because she had intended to buy a parrot, but because it looked so unhappy. Not surprisingly, the insecurity of the previous month made this young parrot extremely clingy. It was so loving that it did not want to leave her or let her out of its sight and this, in itself, created behavioral problems.

Another more serious example was a young cockatoo that had its wings clipped inexpertly. The feathers had been cut straight across, apparently so short that the cut ends were irritating the cockatoo. Instead of playing with its toys, the cockatoo just chewed the cut feather ends— then started pulling out the good feathers. The discomfort of these badly cut feathers must have been constant.

Opposite: *A Quaker, or Monk, Parakeet preening its tail.*

WING CLIPPING

A prospective purchaser should adamantly refuse to buy a parrot with clipped wings. The harmful and incorrect advice is often given that a parrot should be wing-clipped in order to be able to train it or to control its behavior. The decision regarding wing clipping must be with the buyer, not the seller. The new owner of the cockatoo referred to on page 95 thought the bad clip had caused a psychological problem. It could have destroyed the cockatoo's potential as a pet, creating a high risk that it would end up in a "rescue center" before it was 2 or 3 years old. In this case the seller dismissed the complaints and said that the feathers would grow back. Even if they did,

the seller was obviously ignorant of the psychological damage that can be caused and the buyer was lacking in the knowledge necessary to make such an important purchase. The first year with the cockatoo—if the owner had the patience to keep it that long—would not be easy.

If young parrots must be clipped, this should be done after they have spent several months flying and strengthening their wing and pectoral muscles. If their flight feathers are clipped too early, and not allowed to grow again for several years, these parrots might never be able to fly.

The only qualification needed to clip a parrot's wings is experience. To gain this, seek advice from an experienced parrot handler. Vets do not necessarily have experience with clipping. The clip should be gentle and progressive—not one that launches a parrot onto the floor, where it could injure its breast bone. This causes much pain and destroys its confidence, thereby altering its personality. It becomes nervous and nippy. A young parrot, like a child, could be emotionally scarred by a bad experience at an early age.

If the owner of a wing-clipped parrot decides to allow the bird to become full-winged, it is not advisable to have the stumps removed by a vet or other person, as this can cause a tumor or serious damage to the feather follicle that precludes growth from that follicle. Patience will be needed until the molt occurs. A frequently asked question is: "How long will it be before he can fly?" It could be some months: this will depend on how long ago the wing feathers were molted, but remember that the bird does not need to molt all the cut primaries for flight to be possible. A careful watch must be kept on the state of its flight feathers. When cleaning out the cage, check for molted cut primaries. Also, when appropriate, test its powers of flight by moving your hand up and down when the bird is perched on it. This will result in it flapping its wings, and it might even take off!

Reasons not to clip

There are several important reasons why parrots should not have their wings clipped:

- It damages them physically. In addition to not allowing them to exercise in the most natural way, it results in the pectoral muscles failing to develop properly. If the bird's flight feathers are later allowed to grow, it will be a long time before it can fly well, as its pectoral muscles will take months to strengthen.
- It can lead to injury as a result of falling.
- It can result in infection or tumors.
- The stress of wing clipping can often trigger feather plucking and other psychological problems. Many parrots that cannot fly just after being weaned become anxious and fearful.

Trimming the flight feathers

An alternative to a full clip (cutting most of the primary and secondary flight feathers), which is to cut about 1 in. (2.5 cm) off the end of the flight feathers. This prevents a parrot falling and injuring itself, as often happens with a full clip. It also prevents a parrot flying upward. It can still fly down and get some wing exercise, and it is easier to train a parrot, especially in a new environment. When the training is completed, the flight feathers can be allowed to grow.

THE COMPANY OF SENSITIVE PEOPLE

Another factor that will influence a parrot's first year and, perhaps, the rest of its life is the company of gentle and sensitive people who show their parrot nothing but love and respect. If there are children in the family, an adult might be unaware of the fact that the parrot is being teased or harassed in some way. I question the wisdom of acquiring a parrot that will have the company of young children. Children are too fast in their movements, and can be unpredictable and thoughtless in their actions. If a sensitive bird like a Gray Parrot is exposed to such stress early in its life, it can become very nervous.

Obviously, these factors should be taken into consideration before acquiring the bird (see Chapter 2). If the owner is not sufficiently aware of the needs of a parrot to have done so, he or she is unlikely to understand why the young parrot is not living up to expectations. In any case, expectations are often unrealistically high regarding behavior and talking ability. Both require much time and patience. Lack of them can lead to a disillusioned owner.

If the relationship between you and your young parrot is not progressing as you had hoped, don't blame your bird! The fault more likely lies with you. It is true that there are some parrots that do not have the mentality to make good pets. Just because a parrot has been hand-reared does not guarantee that it will be suitable for this purpose. It depends on the temperament of the individual bird, the species, and, to a degree, its sex.

Temperament is not something that can be predicted. Even young from the same nest can have very different personalities. However, some species are less easily stressed, less sensitive, and therefore unlikely to be feather pluckers. In this category is, for example, the Black-headed Caique, which will probably give a trouble-free first year, in contrast to the Gray Parrot. "Why is my African Gray plucking itself?" is a question too often asked by the owner of a young Gray, from 6 months onwards. It is usually difficult to answer this question because the owner never tells you what you need to know or admits that he does not spend enough time with it. He will tell you about its diet, its cage, and its toys, but he has not delved into its psychology—and this is where the answer usually lies. All young parrots need direction—none more so than Grays. Discipline, in the kindest sense, is so important!

Discipline results from teaching simple requests, such as stepping on to your hand.

To spoil a young parrot and let it do whatever it wants because it is so "cute" is not clever. It is extremely foolish, especially with a species as intelligent and manipulative as a Gray.

Below: *Little more than 1 in. (2.5 cm) has been cut from the flight feathers of this Gray Parrot.*

If you let it be in charge, as some indulgent owners do, you are creating a problem that will not be easy to correct. I have seen this happen many times. A parrot that is allowed too much freedom within the house will come to believe that it is practically ruling the household. If it has not received basic training early on (for example, "Step up"; see page 122) it will soon be out of control. This makes life difficult for the people in the house and it can change their attitude toward the bird. Equally serious, a parrot without a guiding hand will suffer psychologically, and feather plucking will often be the result. Most parrots are highly sociable birds, members of a flock in which the adults guide and teach the young. Imagine a human child without anyone to discipline and guide it, growing up without any rules: the child would soon be in all kinds of trouble. So it is with parrots. If you are not firm and do not establish rules, they will have no respect for you.

Below: *You cannot control a parrot, such as this Amazon, when it is on your shoulder.*

SCREAMING AND SQUAWKING

The Gray is among the least noisy of the larger parrots, but many species can make your life hell with their shrieking. Instead of yelling at your parrot (something that no sympathetic owner does), ask yourself one question: "Why is he so noisy?" I refer to persistent shrieking, not the joyous calls parrots use to greet the dawn and sometimes the dusk. This is natural behavior in most species. To some people, the noise level in macaws and cockatoos might be unacceptable, which is why it is so important to hear the calls of a species before you buy, either by visiting a pet store, zoo, bird park, or breeder.

Parrots do not yell and scream for no reason. Often all they need is the reassurance that you are near. Lacking a companion of their own species, they look on their human owner as their mate. Parrots yell to keep in touch with each other. They will keep calling until that call is answered. So do not ignore your bird when it is noisy. You do not have to go to it. Just call out, or speak to it, every time you pass the cage. Continuous calling might be a sign that you are not paying the parrot enough attention. Hand-reared parrots are extremely demanding and need a certain level of attention on a daily basis. A parrot that spends many hours alone during the day is certain to be noisy when its owner returns because it naturally wants his or her company.

Above: *The noise level of macaws could be a problem in many homes.*

Keep them occupied

Many parrots are loud simply because they do not have enough to do. They have active minds and beaks, and both need to be busy. It is not easy to maintain a supply of wood and rope for gnawing, so try to find longer-lasting items. An excellent toy is a small coconut with the milk drained out, attached to a length of chain and hung from the cage roof. Another is small blocks of wood, with a hole in the center of each, threaded onto a chain. Both items are cheap and easy to make. They will provide hours of occupation as well as keeping the beak in trim. Offcuts of pine and other wood commonly used in the home are safe.

Other inexpensive or cost-free objects that will keep your parrot amused are small cardboard boxes, bells, cotton rope ladders, rawhide leather hung up in strips, or thin strips threaded through the cage bars. Short lengths of string, no more than 6 in. (15 cm) long, can be tied to the cage bars. The strands are teased open and nibbled at; longer lengths could be dangerous. A piece of chamois leather tied to the cage is excellent for chewing and for cleaning the beak. It should be washed regularly.

An environment that changes during the day helps to relieve boredom. For example, your

parrot should spend part of the day in a different room on a stand or in a second cage, away from its main cage, perhaps near a big window (but protected from the sun) where it can watch the birds in the garden. Lucky are the companion parrots who have access to an outdoor aviary for part of the day, weather permitting.

An overstimulating environment, such as a family with screaming children or arguing adults, will encourage some parrots, such as Amazons, to add to the cacophony. (Note that the more sensitive parrots, such as Grays and Eclectus, might become stressed in these surroundings.) Television and music with the volume turned up also encourage parrots to make a lot of noise. Need I say that shouting at a parrot to be quiet is a "drama" reward and will only encourage them to be even noisier?

Why parrots are noisy

- Lack of human attention
- Lack of items to keep the beak occupied
- A boring, unchanging environment
- Being left alone for hours every day
- Hunger (in a young parrot)
- An overstimulating environment (frequent or continuous loud sounds)

Opposite: *A small coconut attached to a chain will provide hours of amusement.*

Above right: *Removing nuts from this container is a challenging and time-consuming occupation for a parrot.*

Change the sound

If screaming or squawking is still a problem, concentrate on changing the scream into another sound. For example, Amazons and Grays like to whistle, so by whistling a tune you can usually get them to stop screaming and start whistling. Many Amazons love to sing, so if you sing they will join in. White cockatoos have a well-developed sense of rhythm, so if you clap your hands and sway, they will become alert, stop screaming, and sway in unison. Large macaws are less easy to divert—but do not give them a food treat to stop the screaming or they will learn that screaming earns a reward.

Birds that do not like being sprayed will usually stop screaming when you take out the sprayer.

After you have had your parrot a few weeks, especially if it is an adult bird, you might wonder why it has become much noisier. In fact it has now regained its normal noise level. Moving an older parrot to a new location causes a temporary loss of confidence and quieter behavior.

What should you do if your parrot screams to demand even more attention? This is most likely to happen with a white cockatoo. It has been out of its cage with you, perhaps for an hour. As soon as you put it back, it screams and screams and becomes agitated. The best move is to leave the room immediately after it starts and not to return until it has stopped. This is the only way to teach the bird that screaming has the reverse effect to that desired. If you give in,

Left: *Many cockatoos like to sway to music or to the sound of clapping.*

you are reinforcing the screaming habit. If you have a parrot that behaves like this, put some form of food treat or a fresh-cut piece of apple or willow in the cage before you return it, to divert its attention. However, when you enter the room and the bird is quiet, playing, or resting, praise it and rub its head, if that is what it likes. It will learn to associate this pleasure with its good behavior.

If you are at home all day with your parrot but it screams a lot in the evening, perhaps because you are now dividing your attention between it and your partner, one solution might be to make a heavy dark cover for its cage and cover it up early. This solution is acceptable only if the bird has had plenty of attention during the day. It might not work if it is in the same room. To habitually cover a parrot because it is noisy is wrong. Aim to discover the cause of the problem and correct this—not to shut the parrot out of your life.

You should be aware of the difference between screaming for attention and screaming (or, in the case of Gray Parrots, growling) out of fear. A frightened bird has a different, more urgent tone to its screams. Circumstances that might cause this are someone walking into the room with a big black bag on their shoulder, a strange object placed near the cage or hung on the wall, or, in the case of one conure, a new swing hung in the cage. All such situations can be averted with some

thought. When strangers come to the house, don't let them take large bags or packets into the room where your parrot is, and never allow them to approach the cage and touch it. Permanent items should be introduced as far from the cage as possible, then gradually moved nearer.

For many new parrot owners, the first year is one in which they learn a great deal about their parrot. Look and listen. You will probably discover that your parrot gives you a clue before starting to scream, a certain sound that you will be able to recognize. If you attend to it then, with praise, a head scratch, or something to occupy its beak, the screaming will be diverted. This is just the beginning. It can take most people years to discover all the idiosyncrasies of their parrot. Many never do so because their mind is not receptive to the fact that the parrot is trying to communicate with its human companion. I do not mean in words. The human should be ever observant and never underestimate the parrot's intelligence and abilities. Only in this way can a worthwhile relationship develop.

Forced weaning

What are perceived as behavioral problems by some parrot owners are not such at all. The problem is with the human who lacks sufficient knowledge of parrot behavior and/or psychology. As an example, I was contacted by the owner of a 7-month-old hybrid macaw who was squawking a lot. The owner wrote: "I've tried ignoring him, covering the cage up. Nothing seems to work. Is there anything else I could try? He's 'silly tame' and talks a lot but I can't get him to stop squawking for attention. I'm going out of my mind." My heart went out to this young macaw, a highly sociable and affectionate creature, removed from contact with his own kind and desperately needing a close relationship and a lot of attention. Young macaws are very demanding and will make their presence

felt very loudly indeed if they are unhappy. A young macaw, or any other parrot that has been hand-reared, expects a high level of human attention. If macaws are kept in a domestic situation, they need to be in a household where people are present for all or most of the day, where they can receive almost constant stimulation and attention. Very few people can provide such conditions, which is why most macaws are better off in an outdoor aviary with a member of their own species.

At 7 months a macaw is a real baby. If it was in the wild it would be flying with its parents for almost a year. A young captive macaw left alone for hours each day would feel abandoned, so when its owner returned it would call loudly for attention. Furthermore, most macaws are

Above: *Macaws are better off in an outdoor enclosure with members of their own species.*
Opposite: *The Hyacinthine Macaw, an endangered species, is not an appropriate companion bird.*

force-weaned much too early, perhaps at 16 weeks or so. This leaves them feeling insecure and, in many cases, permanently hungry. Young macaws of large species wean at 5 to 6 months. Thereafter they need much soft food and a lot of food for several months—more than an adult macaw. To try to wean them onto seed or pellets at an early age is extremely detrimental to their health and to their state of mind. Reverting to spoon-feeding every evening (or even more frequently) will indicate how hungry the bird is. A recently weaned parrot should be offered all kinds of soft foods, in addition to fruit, such as warm cooked pasta, vegetables, corn on the cob, and rice and beans.

Spend as many hours as possible with your macaw, sitting quietly talking to it and rubbing its head—while you are watching TV, for example. If you cannot spend at least two hours a day with it, and if it is left alone in the house for five hours or more daily, you might need to consider whether the bird would be better off with someone who can devote more time to it.

BITING

People with a lot of experience with parrots never (or almost never) get bitten. They read the warning signs that indicate that a parrot will bite if provoked further. These signs vary a little according to the species. In some, such as Amazon parrots, they are so obvious, with sufficient time between warning and lunge, that no one should be bitten. The eyes flash, the tail is fanned and the neck feathers are raised. In Gray Parrots, the signs are subtler (a look of concentration with eyes "pinned" or slightly closed) but the bird reacts so quickly that many people are bitten. A defensive posture, with the beak slightly open, is adopted by many parrots, with the body held tense, often with the wings held slightly away from the body. Most parrots would fly rather than bite, but if they are wing-clipped this is impossible; therefore wing clipping can increase aggressive behavior, as can being confined to a small cage.

Common causes

There are two main reasons for biting: to challenge your authority and fear. Refusal to comply with commands, and biting, are typical of young parrots at the age of 1

to 3 years (depending on how quickly the species matures). If they have been trained to respond to basic commands, such as "Step up," it is much easier to cope with this situation. Retraining of this request, and any others they know, will reinforce respect for the owner as flock leader. A parrot does not bite a flock member of senior rank. However, even the tamest, friendliest parrot might nip or bite if you invade its territory or behave in some other inappropriate way.

Opposite: Be vigilant when interacting with a parrot for the first time.

Above: *If you place a parrot on your shoulder, expect to get your ear bitten.*

Respect for your parrot

Just as a parrot must learn what is unacceptable to us, so we must learn what is unacceptable to it. This includes crossing the boundary of its territory, that is, its cage. While it is acceptable to put your hand toward a parrot in a positive manner for it to step up, do not expect it to tolerate removing a toy, for example, while the bird is inside the cage. Such tasks should be carried out when the parrot is elsewhere. You should never have to put your hand inside the cage to remove a food or water container.

If extra containers are needed buy a swing feeder (with two or three containers) and set them into the cage.

Some parrots are so territorial that trying to take them out of the cage is unwise. Placing a stand close to the cage for the parrot to climb on, then moving the stand away from the cage is one answer. Another is to use a perch instead of your hand.

It is not unusual for a parrot to behave in a territorial manner when inside its cage, so that if you put your fingers through the bars to scratch its head or to drop a tidbit into the food container, the parrot will bite you. You are unlikely to change this behavior—so desist!

A parrot will be more likely to bite if you make it do something that it does not like, such as going back into its cage. Then it might quickly turn round and give you a nip. This behavior can probably be averted if you place a favorite tidbit or a different toy in the cage, so that its attention is diverted.

Biting is often unwittingly reinforced by a nervous handler. For example, if an owner goes to pick up the parrot and the parrot lunges and bites, or prepares to bite, and the handler retreats, the parrot has learned that biting (or lunging) achieves the desired result. Often all that is needed is a more positive approach (but not an aggressive or loud approach). A handler who shows confidence is less likely to be bitten. A parrot immediately detects a hesitant manner. Some new owners mistake holding on with the beak for nipping when they are teaching their parrot to "Step up." The parrot reaches forward to steady itself or because it is unsure what to do, the handler moves his fingers away, and the parrot holds on firmly with its beak.

Common situations in which the owner might be bitten are when he or she attempts to remove the parrot from someone else, when the parrot is on the owner's shoulder and someone passes close by, and when the parrot is in a state of excitement. All these situations are avoidable. It is not recommended to permit a parrot to sit on someone's shoulder. Many owners must have been puzzled when a bird in such a position suddenly turned and bit them, apparently for no reason. There is always a reason—and this is usually redirected aggression. What happens is that someone in the room does something that the parrot finds threatening. Unable to bite that person, the parrot bites the person on whose shoulder it is sitting. This means that it bites their cheek or ear or, in the worst scenario, goes for the eye. If the parrot had been sitting on that person's knee, the fact that it was about to bite would have been observed and the bite would have been avoided.

Because you do not have "owl vision," you are blind to the intentions of a bird sitting on your shoulder. A parrot should not be scolded for biting in these circumstances. It is an instinctive reaction, brought about by the owner's ignorance.

After being bitten a few times the owner can lose his confidence in handling his parrot. Therefore the biting issue must be dealt with promptly. The best way to do this is to train the parrot to step onto a small perch or stick. If it wants to bite at the stick this dissipates some of its aggression. The stick should be the length of the parrot or a little longer, preferably of a light color (such as a dowel) and placed near the cage for a day before it is used.

The handler can make sure that stick training is a good experience with praise and a tidbit. After a while, the stick can be used only on occasions as stepping up again becomes part of the normal routine.

Biting out of fear might occur with a phobic bird, or with an untamed wild-caught or parent-reared parrot. It usually happens because the handler is forcing attention on a parrot that is not yet ready for it. The golden rule with such parrots is to let them come to you. This takes a lot of time and more patience than many people possess. In the meantime the bird must receive a lot of attention in the form of human companionship, praise, conversation, and frequent tidbits. The parrot can be let out of its cage if it will return without being caught (and therefore traumatized).

Above: *An owner who fears being bitten can teach a parrot (demonstrated here with a Budgerigar) to step onto a length of dowel.*

PROBLEMS AT ADOLESCENCE

An important aspect of parrot training is to regularly introduce the bird to new situations, objects, and people in order to build and maintain its confidence. This might help to reduce the difficult stage at adolescence that many parrots go through in which they nip and refuse to step up. The age will depend on the species, but this generally occurs between 2 and 4 years. No generalizations can be made regarding the length of time this will last or any other aspect. Even in the same home, in the same species, under the same circumstances, the extent or seriousness of the problem period may vary. It might not happen at all. If it does, reinforcing the training can help to alleviate the problem.

The owner of a male Jardine's Parrot had a hard time with her bird from the age of 12 months for more than a year. He was biting a lot. The key was in carrying out measures to reduce his attitude of dominance. She

Left: *Reinforcing training, such as stepping onto your finger, can solve problems that occur in adolescent parrots.*

lowered his cage by cutting 12 in. (30 cm) off the legs of the table it was on so the cage was below shoulder level. She did not allow him to sit on top of the cage. To reinforce his "Step up" training she took him into a room away from his cage, put him on the back of a chair, and coaxed him to step onto her hand, praising him when he did so. After carrying out this exercise every day for several weeks, he became gentler and his biting occurred only when he was in a bad mood. In this case she would pick him up in a towel and return him to his cage.

One owner of two Maximilian's Pionus, male and female nest mates, had problems with the male when he was about 1 year old. He became highly territorial and attacked her, inflicting nasty bites. Although this phase passed, at the age of 5 years both male and female were capable of temperamental behavior. In *Parrots Magazine*, Amanda Gregory wrote of the male: "He will swing from gentle to ferocious if he is not permitted to do exactly as he wishes."

Another aspect of sexual maturity is that a parrot might try to mate with the perch, with a toy, or with his owner's hand. Despite the advice that is usually handed out, I see nothing wrong with this. It is normal behavior. If you deprive a sexually mature parrot of the company of its own kind, especially hand-reared birds that have never had the chance to socialize with their own species, you should expect this during a period that might last up to a couple of months each year. I do not see this as a problem unless it is associated with aggression toward a human.

PHOBIC BEHAVIOR

This term refers to parrots that have become terrified of something—even of their human companion. The owners usually state they do not know the reason for this. Whatever the reason, the owner's attitude to his or her parrot will almost certainly change subconsciously, probably for the worse. This will make the task of regaining the parrot's trust even more difficult. No matter how tense and upset the owner might be feeling at the parrot's behavior, he or she must exude an air of calm. If a parrot feels that fear has returned, as might happen if it has started to bite, trust-building is impossible. To rebuild trust, a lot of patience and a very caring attitude are essential.

It is advisable to behave in a submissive manner, avoiding eye contact with the parrot and moving around it slowly and quietly. Instead of handling it, spend periods sitting near the parrot, perhaps watching TV or reading, in a quiet and relaxed manner. Patience is essential and no rapid change in its behavior should be expected. It could take weeks before trust is regained. The parrot must want to renew the friendship.

If a parrot suddenly reacts with fear to a person,

it might simply be because they are wearing something unfamiliar or of a color it dislikes. This is not to be confused with persistent phobic behavior. For example, my pet lorikeet refuses to step onto my hand and might even flutter around his cage in fear if I go near him wearing a certain floral top.

FEATHER PLUCKING

Feather plucking is a common problem in the more sensitive species, such as Grays, cockatoos, macaws, and Eclectus Parrots. It is usually associated with ill health (even heavy-metal poisoning), a poor diet, or stress; in the latter category I include lack of discipline. Sometimes young birds, especially Grays, pluck before they are 1 year old. Hand-reared parrots usually become very assertive at this age. If they are not trained to step onto the hand and to go back to the cage when required, they believe that they have control over their human companions. This can cause problems, often including feather plucking.

Plucking might also occur if the parrot does not receive enough focused attention. An intelligent bird like a Gray needs a lot of interaction with people and stimulation. It needs the owner's attention for a couple of hours a day. Because it is often difficult to determine the cause of feather plucking, in the case where there has been no disruption to its normal routine, and no obvious signs of ill health, it is advisable to have the parrot checked by an avian vet, who will be much more aware of the factors that cause feather plucking than a small-animal vet. Blood tests and other tests might also provide clues to the cause.

Feather plucking can be reinforced inadvertently by naive owners. If they immediately pay attention to the parrot and say, "Don't do that!" they are rewarding it for plucking. The best move is to leave the room without a word. It is very important to provide occupation, such as fresh-cut apple branches to gnaw. These might need to be introduced at a distance and gradually moved

Opposite: *The Gray Parrot is a species known for its susceptibility to feather plucking.*
Below: *This Black-headed Caique has plucked some of its breast feathers.*

nearer if they have not been offered before. The same applies to swings and ropes; these can provide hours of amusement.

If this is a long-term problem, it might be impossible to stop it. The feather follicles might have been destroyed, so no new feathers can grow. Vets often recommend the use of a plastic collar fitted around the neck to prevent plucking. This does not address the root of the problem, and plucking will resume as soon as the collar is removed. I believe a collar should be used only if the parrot is making itself bleed. The collar buys time while some kind of therapy is given—perhaps homeopathic remedies to calm it down.

Many of the calls that I receive from worried parrot owners relate to this problem. A typical call related to a 3-year-old Gray Parrot that plucked itself for 18 months. Its owner worked from home, so lack of companionship was not a problem. The Gray was also very friendly with the family's German Shepherd dog. When I asked what the Gray had to keep its beak busy I was told that it never played with toys and was afraid of apple twigs.

Above: *A swing with pellets.*
Left: *If feather plucking is so serious that a parrot makes itself bleed, the use of a collar might be necessary.*
Opposite: *Toys will keep your parrot occupied and help to prevent feather plucking.*

It sat in its cage doing nothing but plucking itself, and had reached the point where it was making itself bleed. I suggested that this was due to not introducing these items at a very early age, but I was wrong. When I asked about diet I was told that the Gray ate only seed. Naturally I offered the usual advice to give only a few grains in the morning with a dish of fruit and vegetables. He had done all this, then offered some seed and scrambled egg at 2 p.m. The result was that during one week the Gray ate only the small amount of seed and refused to sample pellets, fruit, or vegetables, except for grapes. (At least these provided it with some vitamins and calcium.) It was then that the owner himself came up with a solution. The Gray was a much-loved bird and he did not want to part with it, but a friend who kept a Gray was prepared to take his. This seemed to me to offer the best hope of a normal life for this parrot. Kept next to the other Gray, a normal, happy bird, it would watch the other one eating a varied diet and playing with toys and, almost certainly, would eventually copy it.

6

Basic training

Much has been written about training parrots. Some of the advice can leave the reader confused—or even angry at the lack of respect shown by the writer. Sometimes the reader might pick out a few key words on which to hang his or her philosophy. In a single sentence I found a philosophy that all parrot owners would do well to emulate: "The success I have had with my birds is grounded on consistent boundary setting and trust building (something working with elementary school children in deprived areas has successfully prepared me for)."

These words were written by Stephen Bloomfield in *Parrots Magazine*. As a teacher of young children, he already knew the principles of basic training; these are the same for a child as they are for a parrot. If more owners realized this, training would be easier and misunderstandings fewer. Problems arise because owners greatly underestimate parrot intelligence and the need to set boundaries. Without proper parental guidance, children treat no one with respect and scream and make a fuss until they get their own way. Parrots are no different. Instead of being a pleasure they become a nuisance. This is not the fault of the parrots. Sadly, some first-time parrot owners give no more thought to guiding a parrot through those first formative months than if it were a goldfish in a bowl.

Opposite: *Success in training a parrot is based on trust-building.*

HAND-REARED PARROTS

Training should start on acquisition, assuming that the parrot has been hand-reared. Such birds are very easy to handle and handling must be maintained on a daily basis if a parrot is to remain tame and amenable. In any case, a hand-reared parrot desperately needs the close physical contact with a human that it has learned to expect and that is necessary to its well-being in the absence of a companion of its own kind. The first lesson, to step up onto the hand, should be taught from an early age (see page 122).

It is not reasonable to expect a parrot to be amenable to training when it is eating, sleeping, or dozing in the afternoon. At other times it should be so, provided that nothing has happened in the

previous few minutes to upset it. Just as a parrot can observe when a person is nervous or in a bad mood, the owner should also learn to read his or her parrot's state of mind. There are times when a parrot wants to be left alone. The more aggressive species may bite if an attempt is made to handle them then. Gray Parrots are among the least aggressive species, and if a Gray does not welcome human attention at a particular time, it would be more likely to react by firmly clasping its beak around a finger than by biting. But it will bite after it has issued a warning that has been ignored. On the other hand, an Amazon parrot or a macaw is more likely to react by lunging and perhaps biting. So the first rule relating to training is that the parrot should be in a receptive state of mind.

The next point to consider is where the training will be carried out. The best location is in a room or an area with few distractions and away from its cage. You might want to take your parrot into the hall and sit it on the back of a chair. If this is unfamiliar territory, first let the parrot look around to get its bearings.

Opposite: *The first lesson, to step up onto the hand, should be taught from an early age.*
Right: *Train your parrot: take it to an unfamiliar area and place it on the back of a chair or teach it to step onto some apple-wood branch.*

Stepping up

In the aspects of discipline and safety, it is imperative that a parrot can be moved in and out of its cage, or away from an unsuitable place, at any given time. If a parrot has to be chased to catch it, this indicates that there is no relationship between parrot and owner or that the bird is in control. If a parrot is trained to perform only one command, it must be to step on and off the hand.

It is easy for a young bird to learn this, and so simple with a hand-reared parrot. Place it in the training area, on its stand, or on the back of a chair. Speak to it kindly and move your hand at medium speed, and not jerkily, toward its abdomen. Push your index and middle finger (or index finger only in a small bird) firmly above its legs. Your hand must be at an angle that allows the bird to step up, as this is much easier than stepping down. Say "Up!"

If it steps onto your hand, praise it. If it does not, gently place its feet on your fingers. You can then transfer the bird to your other hand, repeating "Up!" You should do this three or four times. Replace the bird on the stand or chair, saying "Down!" Praise it again. Repeat the process a few minutes later. Repeat this each time

1

you take the bird out of its cage. It will soon learn. When it does it automatically as you place your fingers above its feet, continue to say "Up!" It will not be long before the bird starts to step onto your hand as soon as you say "Up!" After teaching a parrot to step up, the word "Down!" should be used so the parrot is aware of what will follow. Praise should be given because most tame parrots do not want to be put down.

If teaching this is difficult because your parrot does not step up and it is not tame enough for you to gently move its foot onto your hand, what should you do? I would suggest repeating the exercise using a piece of thick dowel. Eventually a shorter piece of dowel can be used, and then dispensed with. If this also fails after a number of attempts, it is probable that the parrot needs more time to adjust to its new environment and to trust you before training recommences. Under no circumstances shout at the bird or do anything to cause it to fear you, or training will be difficult in the future. Always be calm and patient.

After the "Step up" training or stick training has been achieved, do not leave the cage door open for the bird to come out when it wishes. Wait for

1. *To teach your parrot to step up, place two fingers above its legs, against its abdomen, and push gently.*
2. *Praise the bird when it steps up.*

2

a suitable time, and then invite it to step onto your hand, using the word "Up!" If the parrot is feeding, playing, or sleeping, wait a few minutes. It is your decision when it comes out. It is important to use these commands throughout your bird's life. If you cease to handle the parrot you cannot expect it to stay tame and to respond to the command. Handling your parrot is imperative for its happiness. It needs that contact with you.

Suppose you acquire an adult parrot that has never been taught to step up, or you neglected to train your bird when it was young. Will you be able to teach it? The answer is yes, in most cases, although this might be difficult with a very mature bird and a different approach might be

necessary. With a tame bird it should not be too difficult. With a cockatoo it would be easy because the "Up!" command could be followed by a cuddle, something that no *Cacatua* species is likely to refuse. With a bird that is not tame it is necessary to wait until some kind of rapport has been established, then use food as an incentive.

Averting unwanted behavior

"No!" is a command with which a parrot should be familiar. For example, as your parrot reaches out to tear a strip of wallpaper off the wall or to nibble at a curtain, this is the word that should stop it in its tracks! It is true that it will probably do it anyway when you are not looking, but the point is that the bird understands what you do not want it to do! Remember that parrots are very clever and can divert your attention when requested to do something they do not wish to do. The most common trick is to put their head down for a scratch. Don't fall for this one!

Left: *Orange, a favorite food of the Blue and Yellow Macaw, can be used as a training reward.*
Opposite: *This Umbrella Cockatoo has been taught to wave goodbye.*

WILD-CAUGHT PARROTS

Someone who inherits or rescues an untrained wild-caught parrot must take an entirely different approach that focuses on winning the bird's trust. Many parrots that were taken from the wild after being trapped, rather than removed from the nest, never lose their fear of hands, or take years to do so. They have long memories, and the memory of the cruel treatment and rough handling they received never fades.

Every movement around such a bird must be calm and unthreatening. Avoid eye contact until it is more at ease in your presence. Hold your hands behind your back and talk to the parrot often. When it learns not to move away, remove the food container from the cage for a few minutes and offer treats. If you are tall, do not loom over your parrot as this is threatening; sit so that you are at its level when giving tidbits or training. Spend time near your parrot, perhaps just

reading, to show you are not a threat.

A tame, but untrained, wild-caught bird will not always respond to all forms of training. For example, a Goffin's Cockatoo, over 26 years old, was taught to "Step up" and would willingly do so when removed from her cage or other objects. However, she refused to comply when she was on a person. A compromise was found by teaching her to step onto a cushion. A dowel or a parrot ladder could also have been useful.

A friend described the progress she made with a wild-caught Gray Parrot acquired soon after it was imported. At first he threw himself about the cage in fear whenever she went near. After a year he had calmed down a lot and would even sit on the back of her chair when he was let out, but as soon as she moved her hands he would fly away. She told me: "He desperately wants physical contact but is still too afraid of hands."

WORKSHOPS AND BEHAVIORISTS

In the past, advertisements in magazines by self-styled "parrot behaviorists" were not uncommon. If you contact such a person, ask about their qualifications. A genuine behaviorist will at least have a degree in human psychology (this can be applied to parrots). If they have no qualifications, my advice would be not to use their service. Some unqualified people have given quite appalling advice.

True behaviorists teach parrot owners how to reinforce good behavior and to observe what occurred right before the desired behavior took place. With this knowledge undesirable behavior can be eliminated. In some cities, workshops are held with genuine experts who explain how to train parrots, often resulting in success after a short time. Mornings are devoted to lectures and afternoons to practical, "hands-on" training.

TEACHING BY EXAMPLE

Most parrots learn more quickly, and lose their fear when they see another parrot happily being handled by a human. One parrot owner, Dot Schwarz, rescued a wild-caught Timneh Gray that had been kept in a laundry room, alone and terrified, and was then given to a rescue center. She called the bird Mirt and kept her in an aviary, where she had much interaction with the other parrots, including another Timneh called Timi.

Mirt would not allow a human near her and would bite if she felt threatened. After withdrawing sunflower seed from their diet, Dot encouraged Timi to land on her left hand to take the seeds. After 14 days, Mirt followed suit, frightened though she was at first.

Another parrotkeeper, Priscilla Old, had experienced problems with her 5-year-old Gray Parrot, Sparkle, when taking her out of the cage. Sparkle would hang on the door, put her head down to be scratched or, if she was in a bad mood, she

Left: *Parrots, such as these young Timneh Grays, learn from each other.*

would strike out. It was difficult to persuade her to step onto her owner's hand so that she could be placed on her play stand. After attending a workshop with the famous trainer Steve Martin, Priscilla was determined to solve this problem. When Sparkle refused to come out, Priscilla showed her the perch she wanted her to stand on, and then held a pine nut near the side of the cage. Sparkle turned her back and returned to the cage to hang upside down. Priscilla went to the next parrot, another Gray, took her out,

reinforced the good behavior with a pine nut, and put her on her stand. She left the room, and when she returned Sparkle was standing on the desired perch within the cage. She asked Sparkle to step up; Sparkle complied and Priscilla took her to her stand, with much praise, and gave her a pine nut. It was so easy!

FLIGHT COMMANDS

If your parrot is full-winged, you should teach it some simple flight commands. Training should start when the parrot is young, or very soon after you acquire it. If taught at an early age it should always be easy to control. Teaching flight commands not only reinforces discipline at an early age, it also ensures the bird's safety in an emergency.

Calling your bird

As a recently weaned bird that is discovering its flight potential, your parrot will naturally want to fly to you. To encourage it to do so, hold your outstretched arm high and call "Come!" If it does not fly to you at first, be patient, and hold up a treat. When it flies to you, praise it enthusiastically and give it the treat. After a while, you could withhold the treat, but give its head a scratch (if this is what it likes). The bird will soon learn this if the request to "Come!" always accompanies your outstretched arm. Parrots are very clever, so you need to outsmart them! Do not use this command only when you want to put the parrot back in his cage or it will associate it with something bad. Spend a few minutes making a fuss over it before you put it back.

It is easy to train a young, hand-reared parrot to fly to you. Simply extend your arm toward the bird and wait for it to land on your arm.

Preventing takeoff

There will be times when you do not want your parrot to fly to you or another person. To start training it not to fly, you will need to observe those signs, including the slightly crouched posture that indicates it is preparing for takeoff. When you see this, hold up your hand with the palm showing and the fingers outspread and call out "Stop!" It might try to land on your shoulder, but this will be impossible if you spread the palm of each hand in front of and just above your shoulder.

At first it will not understand, but as soon as it realizes what you want and aborts takeoff, praise it lavishly and perhaps offer it a little treat.

You might not need to use this request very often, so practice it three or four times a week when the bird's training is complete. If possible, ask another family member to assist in this training. In this way you will be able to stop it flying to a stranger or someone who is afraid of parrots.

To train a parrot not to land on you, raise your hands, palms up, on either side of your face, and call out "Stop!"

RETURNING YOUR PARROT TO ITS CAGE

Many young parrots will naturally object to being returned to their cage. They are enjoying themselves and have no wish to be caged up again. They will refuse to step up and may fly away. Being put back should therefore be associated with something good. You might offer your parrot its favorite food when it returns to its cage and at no other time. With some species, cage time might be made into a game. For example, white cockatoos have a marked sense of rhythm. If you sway from side to side and clap your hands, a cockatoo will jerk its head in and out in time and perhaps open its wings as well. A cockatoo will love the focus of attention from a clapping and dancing session that could follow being returned to its cage. Alternatively, you might have a cuddle session with your parrot and then, while it is in a calm mood, put it straight back into the cage.

Left: *Rewarding your parrot with attention immediately after you return it to its cage will encourage it to enter.*

It is wise to vary the technique used! Always give praise when the parrot goes back in.

Do not try to return your parrot to its cage when it is in an excitable mood or when it is in a high place. Wait for it to come down lower. If a parrot is in the habit of perching up high, out of your normal reach, it is a good idea to make a small wooden ladder. You can reach up with the ladder and your parrot is more likely to climb on this than onto your hand.

If your parrot is not tame, but must be returned to the cage at short notice, try to drop a towel over it. Then position the parrot in the towel so that you can place your thumb and forefinger on either side of its upper mandible. This will prevent you from being bitten. If necessary, in the case of a large parrot, put your other hand around its body so that you are gripping it securely (but not tightly) and keeping its feet within the towel. Many parrots have very sharp claws that can lacerate you!

If you must remove an untamed parrot from its cage, it will probably cling to the bars. Put a towel around it, as described, and ask someone else to unhook its claws from the bars.

CLICKER TRAINING

Some people use a clicker to train dogs and parrots. A clicker is a small object that makes a clicking sound when pressed, and can be bought from pet stores. It is a signaling device that serves to focus the parrot's attention on what it is being requested to do. At first the clicker should be out of sight, perhaps held behind the trainer's back, and it should never be held close to the bird. Sue Macer, a parrot owner who used this method to train her parrots, wrote in *Parrots Magazine*: "I view it as a humane, non-threatening, trust-building method of teaching basic behaviors, such as stepping up and stepping down, going in and out of a cage, dealing with aggression or screaming, among others, which can be used with any bird no matter how old it is, or how badly it may have been abused by its former owners … The first step is to teach your bird that whenever he hears the click he will be given a reward."

The usual reward in parrot training is a favored, healthy item of food such as a nut. With some parrots a head scratch might be a better incentive. Macer recommends giving an extra-special treat every now and then to keep the parrot's interest and to add to the element of fun. A long-handled spoon can be used to offer a reward to an aggressive or nervous parrot. Leave this spoon near the cage for a couple of days before using

it. When the bird understands that the clicking sound means a reward will follow, you will have its undivided attention! Finish each training session with a successful move, praise your parrot lavishly, and give it a treat.

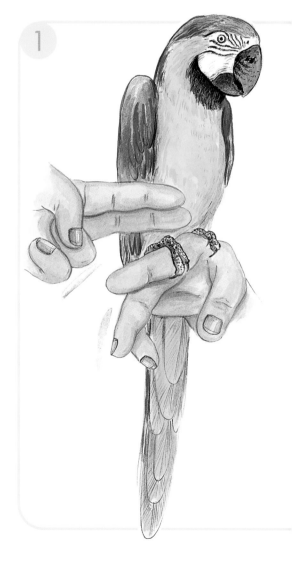

1

SHAKING HANDS

If you have one of the larger parrot species, you might want to teach it a trick or two. Most parrots enjoy learning, and the time you spend with your parrot in such activities strengthens the bond between you and increases the chance of its being well-behaved over the long term.

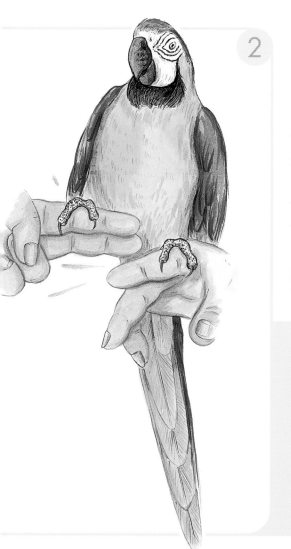

You might, for example, want to teach it to shake hands. When the bird is perched on your hand, hold the first two fingers of your other hand just above one of its feet. (Note whether your bird is right-footed or left-footed by observing which foot it uses to hold food items. Hold your fingers above the preferred foot.) To prevent it from stepping up, do not hold your hand in the usual way, but present two fingers and tuck the other fingers and thumb into your palm. Give the instruction: "Shake hands." The parrot might try to "Step up" (see pages 122–123), so encourage it to hold the end of your finger with its foot. If it does so, gently and slowly move your finger up and down, repeating "Shake hands!" Praise the bird all the time it manages to do this. It will be uncertain what is expected, so keep praising it. When it has accomplished this, do not encourage other people to try it (except family members) because it might bite them.

1. *To teach your parrot to shake hands, offer two fingers and tuck the other fingers into your palm.*
2. *Encourage it to hold your two fingers, then move the fingers up and down, repeating "Shake hands."*

TEACHING TO "TALK"

There is a downside to the miraculous power of mimicry possessed by many parrots. While your parrot might amuse your friends with its ability to copy human speech, it might drive family members almost to insanity by imitating your neighbor's car alarm or copying the ring of the telephone with such accuracy you truly cannot distinguish it from the real thing. One owner of a Gray Parrot was at her wit's end trying to cope with the piercing dog whistle that the bird had learned to imitate in her absence. As she had an ear problem that was seriously aggravated by this high-pitched whistle, she was despairingly considering trying to find a new home for her Gray. Who would want such a bird, however? Think carefully about what you teach your parrot or the sounds to which you expose it. If it imitates the wrong sounds and you are no longer able to keep it, its future might be in jeopardy. This is especially the case if you teach your parrot obscenities.

Scientists believe the ability of parrots to imitate sounds indicates the importance of vocalization to form bonds within a social group or to advertise sexual availability, such as birdsong. In the case of parrots, mimicry is connected with the strong desire to form a bond. Often, owners' expectations are unrealistically high regarding behavior and talking ability. Both require much time and patience. Lack of them can lead to a disillusioned owner—especially when the parrot has been bought for all the wrong reasons.

The worst reason for buying a parrot is the desire to have one that "talks." To buy a parrot because it is capable of mimicry is wrong. It should be revered for the wonderful creature it is, not for doing something a machine can do. Love it for the fact that it is so different from a human being! Instead of being intent on teaching it our language, listen to its vocalizations and try to understand what they mean. You will find that certain sounds are used consistently in certain situations. They might mean that your bird is asking for a piece of the food you are preparing or eating, or that it wants to come out of its cage or go back in.

Because Gray Parrots have the reputation of being excellent talkers, many people interested in this quality buy a Gray as their first parrot, with no understanding that it is far more demanding to keep than a cat or a dog. Many Grays do not utter a word until they are about 12 months old. This is certainly a source of disillusionment to someone who is primarily interested in talking ability. Some Grays do start to mimic as early as 6 months, but this is late compared with some neotropical parrots. Many of these birds have uttered their first word before they are even weaned! When you hear your parrot attempting to mimic the phrase or word, repeat it, and then praise it. Using the same principle, some parrots will learn to whistle tunes. This is especially the case with species such as Grays, for whom whistling sounds are part of the natural range of vocalizations.

Talking ability is dependent on two main factors: natural aptitude and a stimulating environment with sympathetic people. An unhappy parrot will not learn to talk. No true parrot lover will place undue emphasis on the ability to mimic. Does it really matter? Far more important is a good relationship between parrot and caregiver—such as that which exists between my Yellow-fronted Amazon and myself. Her entire vocabulary, after 38 years with me, consists of five words, probably because I never tried to teach her anything! To me, the joy of parrotkeeping is not in what I can teach a parrot but in what it can teach me. A receptive owner never stops learning!

Below: *The Gray Parrot is renowned for its ability to mimic.*

7

Feeding for health and longevity

The first few months after purchase are extremely important for a parrot's diet. Young parrots must not be quickly weaned onto hard foods, such as seed and pellets. They need a large proportion of soft foods. They can then adjust to a diet of harder foods at their own pace.

Every owner would be wise to purchase an electronic scale that weighs to the nearest ½ ounce (14 g), to weigh a young parrot every week and note its weight. Those that have been force-weaned before purchase, not offered enough soft foods, or are not as healthy as their appearance suggests will be underweight and/or losing weight. It is difficult to know what the normal weight should be. The weight of healthy adult Grays, for example, can vary between 14 ounces (400 g) and 19 ounces (525 g), according to the sex, how the bird was reared, and individual circumstances. However, its weight should remain stable from the time it is about 7 months old. Weighing is a quick and easy health check—although it will be easy only if you have made this a routine since the parrot was very young. Some people incorporate a perch into their scale and the parrot can be taught to "Step down" onto this perch.

Opposite: *Beware! The peanuts contained in parrot mixtures are often of poor quality or contain dangerous toxins.*

If you have a young parrot that is losing weight, do not seek advice from a dozen different people, go straight to an avian vet. He or she is the only one who can perform the tests that will reveal if poor health is to blame. If such tests reveal no abnormalities, the diet and possible causes of stress must be examined. It is not easy to overfeed a young parrot as, at the growing stage, it needs to eat more than an adult. This is especially true of young macaws. It would be easy to underfeed them if the rations are based on what an adult would eat.

While many large macaws will eat nuts to the exclusion of all other foods if permitted, no parrot should be totally reliant on one food type in case of problems with its supply. From a nutritional aspect, nuts are a complete food for macaws, although commercially produced nuts do not necessarily offer the same food values as nuts eaten in the wild. An explanation of the types of fat is given later in this chapter (see page 150), but this should not be interpreted in human terms, where polyunsaturated fats are recommended to keep down cholesterol levels. It is believed that Hyacinthine Macaws need nuts containing saturated fats, such as macadamias, Brazils, and fresh coconut, as these equate to the palm nuts they eat in the wild.

Safe food storage is extremely important. Nuts should be stored in dry, dark places because they oxidize (turn rancid) more rapidly when stored in the light. Airtight containers are recommended for storing small quantities, or large containers with tight-fitting lids for larger quantities. Nuts store better in the shell. They will last for years in a freezer.

Left: *Nuts should be limited in the diet of Amazon parrots; unlike macaws, they do not need such high-fat foods.*

FOOD ADDICTION

Correct feeding is not only about quantity; it also relates to feeding appropriate foods to the species in question. From an early age Amazon parrots, for example, must only receive limited amounts of sunflower seed to prevent the development of an addiction that can lead to their becoming overweight, especially if clipped wings mean that they don't get enough exercise. In contrast, you can give a large macaw as much sunflower seed and as many nuts as it can eat, and it is unlikely to become overweight, because most of the large species evolved on a high-fat palm nut diet. It is all too easy to give in to the food addictions of young parrots. In doing so, however, you are reinforcing eating habits that will be extremely difficult to break in later life. Some parrots do have strange preferences, but if their diet appears to be otherwise balanced, you don't need to be concerned. If you have a young

Dietary recommendations

As an approximate guide to diets for different species kept as companion birds (and not for breeding purposes), I would suggest the following, expressed as percentages:

SPECIES	SEED & PELLETS	FRUIT	VEGETABLES & GREEN FOOD	LEGUMES
Gray Parrot	65	20	10	5
Poicephalus	60	20	10	10
Amazons, Pionus				
Small macaws	60	15	15	10
Large macaws (+ 5% nuts)	60	20	5	10
White cockatoos				
(+ 2% nuts)	70	13	15	0
Galahs (small seeds)	70	10	20	0
Budgerigars & Cockatiels				
(seed only)	87	3	10	0

Above: *This female Eclectus has eaten a corn cob, and only the leaves remain to be shredded.*

Amazon that only wants to eat sunflower seeds, you or the previous owner are to blame for giving in to it. Young parrots must be trained to eat a good variety of foods. The length of their lives might depend on it. Dietary deficiencies are at the root of so many diseases. You must train your parrot to eat a healthy diet because this is certainly not something it can learn by itself.

Right from the outset, ban human foods that are harmful and impress on other members of the family that they are taboo. If you never provide them, your parrot will not feel deprived. If you are eating something unhealthy, such as potato chips, do not do so when your parrot is free in the room. If it is in its cage, give it a healthy treat at this time. Avoid the formation of habits that can be difficult to break in later life. Remember that if a parrot wants something, it will not be quiet until it gets it— and this creates conflict.

SUPPLEMENTS

Many opinions have been published regarding diets for parrots, but the fact is that the nutritional requirements of the various species are poorly understood. What is published is usually the result of trial and error or the results of a few food trials on a limited number of species. What is known is that deficiencies of Vitamin A cause the death of many parrots, and equally serious in Gray Parrots is a deficiency of calcium or an imbalance of calcium and Vitamin D. Many parrot owners provide supplements, especially vitamins, but for parrots on an appropriate diet these should be unnecessary. The problem is that the majority of parrots do not eat a suitable diet (although they might be offered one). Therefore parrot owners should carefully assess what their parrots actually eat before putting supplements into the food. The exception is calcium, which is needed by all Gray Parrots and by laying females of all species.

DIETARY DEFICIENCIES

How does an owner know if his or her bird's diet is deficient? In the early stages of deficiencies this will not be obvious, but the parrot's health might deteriorate slowly over a period of several years. Because of the slow deterioration, the owner might not realize that something is wrong until the bird suffers a serious condition, such as a respiratory infection or a rhinolith in the nostril (see Chapter 8). Long-term deficiencies that are not treated can lead to liver and kidney disease, heart disease, seizures, gout, and many other conditions and, finally, death. This is why I am emphasizing the importance of an adequate diet.

An approximate guide to diets for different species kept as companions (not for breeding birds) is given on page 139.

SYMPTOMS OF A POOR DIET

A dietary deficiency can cause feathers to be retained in their sheaths. This problem sometimes occurs on the tail feathers of large macaws. Supplementing their diets with Vitamin B might help.

A molt that produces abnormally colored feathers—for example, light brown feathers in a Gray Parrot that should be gray—might indicate malnutrition. Some confiscated Gray Parrots in my care that were suffering from malnutrition had dark gray feathers with a violet sheen. The color returned to normal when they were given a nutritious diet. It should be noted that a green parrot whose feathers are replaced with yellow, orange, or red feathers might be suffering from kidney or liver disease. In newly imported wild-caught parrots it is common to see dull plumage, with the feathers margined with black. This is probably due to a combination of stress and poor diet, plus the effect of being kept without access to a bath.

SEED

Only species adapted to live in dry environments, such as Budgerigars, Cockatiels, and Galahs, will thrive on a diet that consists mainly of small seeds such as canary and millet. Other species fed on dry seed that forms more than about 80 percent of the diet will suffer health problems over the long term. Dry seed is deficient in protein, vitamins, minerals, and trace elements such as iodine and manganese. (This is why iodine nibbles are made for Budgerigars.) For parrots that come from more humid environments, where food is abundant and varied, seed should form no more than 50 percent of the diet. Seed must be offered fresh daily and the container should be emptied daily (and washed) or it will contain more and more debris and husks until the bird goes hungry. Provide seed mixtures in a small container or only partly fill a large container with them. If not, most parrots will gorge themselves on sunflower seeds. Not only is this wasteful and expensive, it means that the bird will ignore other seeds and healthy fruits and vegetables. There should be at least three containers in the cage: for seed or pellets, fruits and vegetables, and water.

Look carefully at the quality and cleanliness of the seeds you buy. Test every batch of new seed containing sunflower. Examine the size of the kernel; it should fill the husk, and the seed should be fairly plump, unless it is a small variety. Also taste it. A germination test can be made by soaking a small quantity of seed, then leaving it in a warm place to sprout. At least 70 percent of the seed should germinate. If it does not, return it to the supplier. If necessary, buy elsewhere.

Below: *Pumpkin seeds, mung beans for sprouting, and hemp seeds.*
Opposite: *A mixture containing dried fruits, grains, and nuts.*

Seed mixtures

Obtain a mixture with a wide variety of items, as this reduces the possibility of a dietary deficiency. Each one will have different constituents. A varied mixture might contain the following: sunflower seed (striped, white, and/or black), safflower, hemp, melon or pumpkin seed, paddy rice, millet, wheat, banana chips, dried elderberries and rosehips, dried pineapple, raisins, corn, mung beans, flaked peas, and chili peppers, also nuts, depending for which parrots the mixture was formulated. Some mixtures also contain a few pellets or some kind of kibble.

Although such mixtures are a vast improvement over the traditional type, which consisted mainly of sunflower seeds, many still contain items that almost no parrots will eat, such as hard corn and flaked peas. It is suggested that you remove the corn and throw it in a saucepan when vegetables are being cooked; then it might be palatable! All mixtures for larger parrots contain peanuts; these are not recommended. Bear in mind that most parrots are unlikely to eat all these items, so there will be a little waste, but do not put too much seed in the container.

Many parrots, from cockatoos and Amazons to parakeets and *Trichoglossus* lorikeets, enjoy eating millet sprays, which keeps them occupied—and it is a more natural way of feeding than taking food out of a container. Likewise, in summer and fall, the same species will greatly enjoy seeding dock.

Seed values

Parrotkeepers should know which seeds are high in fat and protein. Approximate values in percentages are as follows:

SEEDS	PROTEIN	FAT/OIL
Canary	14–17	5–8
Millet	12	4
Hemp	20	32
Nigella	22	40
Sunflower	23	49
Safflower	16	38
Pumpkin	24	46

PELLETS AND EXTRUDED FOODS

These foods are useful for those parrots that cannot be persuaded to eat much fresh food. I believe that processed food, such as pellets and extruded foods, are no healthier for parrots than they are for humans, and should be offered as no more than about 70 percent of the diet.

Pellets

Pellets might be appropriate for parrot owners who keep perhaps a single bird and are not well informed about dietary needs, as their use avoids serious dietary deficiencies. However, fruits and vegetables should form at least 20 percent of the diet. Pellets were originally formulated for com-

mercially produced livestock such as poultry, whose lifespan is very short. In comparison, parrots can live for 50 years. No one knows the long-term effect of existing on a diet of processed food over such a long period. The advantage is that pellets contain Vitamin A and calcium and probably present a more balanced diet than that received by many parrots. Those who feed pellets should be aware that they contain the necessary vitamins and, under most circumstances, sufficient calcium for pet birds.

Additives are promoted so vigorously that pet owners, anxious to provide the best in nutrition, might be supplying excesses by giving additives. As an example, an excess of Vitamin A causes bone abnormalities, damage to the parathyroid gland, and even kidney and liver damage.

Certain parrots might convert fairly easily to eating pellets—or at least to one brand of organic pellets. Some types are more palatable than others; those that are highly scented or colored might be looked upon with suspicion. Also, some parrots react badly to eating pellets with artificial coloring. The safest pellets are organic; they are

Left: *The long-term effect of feeding pellets to parrots is unknown.*

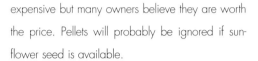

Right: *An example of the worst kind of parrot mixture—mainly sunflower seeds, inedible hard corn, and potentially harmful peanuts.*

expensive but many owners believe they are worth the price. Pellets will probably be ignored if sunflower seed is available.

Extruded foods

Extruded foods are manufactured by adding water and steam to ingredients that have been briefly cooked. It is claimed that using this method makes the nutrients more readily available to the birds and that the food is more digestible. The temperature used in the extrusion process is in excess of 300°F (150°C), and it is claimed that most germs present in food are killed during this process.

Manufacturers state that all the necessary food elements are present in the right proportions, thus parrots on these diets eat one-third less than when offered other foods. It is not explained how the elements can be present in the right proportions when different species (even those within the same genera) have different dietary needs. Some companies produce a range of extruded foods, formulated for different types of birds (large parakeets and parrots).

People who feed pellets and extruded foods must be aware that it is important that clean drinking water is always available. When using such foods initially parrotkeepers must check how much is eaten. Some parrots and parakeets have literally starved to death rather than eat them. In my opinion they should not be fed to species such as Budgerigars that might not recognize them as food and whose dietary needs are, in any case, met so easily.

NUTS

Nuts make excellent foods for parrots, but bear in mind that they are high in fat and should be fed sparingly to species that gain weight easily (see page 139). Nuts are a good source of energy, with over 200 calories per ounce in some varieties. Most nuts are a complete source of protein, and they contain significant amounts of important trace minerals such as iron, calcium, phosphorus, potassium, and magnesium, as well as Vitamins B, C, thiamine, niacin, folacin, pantothenic acid, and alphatocopherol, an antioxidant. Certain commercially available nuts approximate more closely to natural food sources (of macaws, for example), than any other items we can offer.

Walnuts

Walnuts (genus *Juglans*) contain about 63 percent fat, 14 to 15 percent protein, and 16 to 18 percent carbohydrate, also small amounts of Vitamin A, thiamine, riboflavin, and niacin. The quality of walnuts in the shell is good if you buy the "new season" crop. Stale ones can be shriveled and useless. If you use large quantities seek out a wholesaler and buy them by the sack.

For macaws and cockatoos, opening the nut is half the fun, and this can keep them occupied for some time. They insert the tip of the upper mandible into the small opening at the top and prise the nut open. For small macaws, Amazons, and other parrots, the walnuts must be opened. The best method is to insert the tip of a sharp knife into the tiny opening and twist. Macaws love to crunch up walnut shells, and smaller parrots appreciate walnut halves or broken walnuts out of the shell. If available, you can feed whole green walnuts, straight off the tree, complete with shell.

Pecans

The pecan tree (*Carya illinoensis*) is closely related to the walnut. Researchers have found pecans to be a good source of healthy oleic acid. These thin-shelled nuts are also rich in vitamins, minerals, cancer-fighting components, and fiber. Walnuts and pecans contain more Vitamin A than Brazils and pine nuts, for example.

Brazil nuts

Nuts of the Brazil tree (*Bertholettia excelsa*) are expensive because they cannot be grown in plantations. These nuts are a perfect food for Blue and Yellow and Green-winged Macaws, for whom nuts form the most important item of diet in the wild. Brazils contain nearly 70 percent fat and 14 to 17 percent protein. The high fat content means that they should never be offered to species (such as Amazons) that are prone to obesity. It seems likely that Brazil nuts contribute to healthy plumage and skin in macaws and, equally important, they provide occupation and beak exercise. These nuts

are the highest natural source of selenium, an essential trace element whose absorption is enhanced by the nut's valuable amino acid content of cysteine and methionine.

Almonds

Certain parrot species, especially the Palm Cockatoo, are very fond of almonds (*Prunus dolcis*). Do not allow parrots to eat wet almonds (perhaps after they have been dunked in the water pot) because the hydrocyanic acid they contain increases to lethal levels when mature nuts become damp.

A smaller parrot will amuse itself with almonds for hours before it finally penetrates their shells.

Macadamia nuts

The nuts of macadamias (*Macadamia* species), native to Australia and introduced to Hawaii, are readily available. The oil content is about 65 to 75 percent. The shell is very smooth and I believe that only the three largest species of macaw can crack them.

Pine nuts

Many parrots relish the pine nuts available commercially. However, these should be offered in moderation because the supply tends to be erratic. At least two types are available, the large Russian nuts and the smaller Chinese. It is important to open a sample from a new consignment to check the quality and to examine them for exterior mold. An alternative is to buy pine kernels from health-food stores. The fat content is nearly as high as sunflower seed, so feed in moderation to species that easily gain weight.

Palm nuts

The African oil palm (*Elaeis guineensis*) has become a major source of cooking oil worldwide and I believe that its fruit is the only palm fruit that is available commercially. In recent years, these fruits have been exported for parrots; many owners of Gray Parrots and macaws purchase them. However, they need to be stored in a refrigerator and they are expensive.

Palm-fruit extract

This is the unrefined residue (filtered to remove solids) from the pressing process that extracts the oil. It contains polyunsaturated, monounsaturated, and saturated fatty acids, also essential substances such as linoleic acid that are natural antioxidants. It is a major source of beta-carotene, the precursor of Vitamin A. It contains 15 to 300 times more beta-carotene than carrots and green vegetables. Vitamin A is an extremely important component of the diet of most parrot species, including Grays, Amazons, and *Pionus*. It promotes healthy mucus membranes (preventing sinus conditions) and healthy skin. The extract is also said to be a valuable source of Vitamin E (an antioxidant and promoter of fertility). It will improve feather condition and general health. It is inexpensive and, at a recommended teaspoonful (15 ml) per day, a 16-ounce (500 ml) jar is said to last a single bird for six months. Many parrots like to eat it on toast. For smaller species it can be added to the toast (but never to the seed). Palm-fruit extract is a new product, but would appear to be one that will be invaluable in maintaining parrots in good health over the long term.

Coconut

The white meat of the coconut (*Cocos nucifera*) is a great favorite with Hyacinthine and other macaws. Many other parrots, such as Amazons, also like it. Bear in mind the percentage of fat (33 percent), which is not as high as sunflower seed but still high.

Peanuts

The peanut (*Arachis hypogaea*) is a seed with a thin shell that grows underground. It is potentially one of the most dangerous foods that we can offer parrots, yet hardly any parrot mixture is without it. I stopped feeding peanuts to parrots 30 years ago when a beloved bird died of liver disease, almost certainly as the result of eating peanuts. Peanuts often contain aflatoxins. This contamination is common in cereal grains and nuts and is produced by molds, often as the result of careless storage. It is believed that many cases of cancer in humans result from aflatoxin contamination. It is so dangerous that poultry fed on such contaminated food for only a few days can develop malignant tumors. Because peanuts used by most bird food companies are not human grade, the danger is increased many times. However, if you feel you must feed peanuts, I would suggest that you use only human grade nuts and open at least 20 percent of them to check their condition.

Incidentally, no parrots should be offered salted peanuts, as too much salt is harmful. However, unsalted peanut butter (offered on toast) is a great favorite with many parrots. Its oil content is high, in the region of 50 percent, and it also contains about 26 percent protein. It can even be added to homemade hand-rearing foods of chicks of parrot species, such as macaws, that need extra fat, and those that require extra protein when molting or breeding.

Above: *Coconut.*

Opposite: *Pine nuts.*

MINERAL & VITAMIN VALUES

Food Source	Cal	Prot	Carbo	Fat	Water	Ca	Phos	Vit A	Vit C	Lys	Meth
Brazil	656	14%	13%	66%	3%	176mg	600mg	0	0.7mg	0.54mg	1.01mg
Walnut	642	14%	18%	61%	4%	94mg	317mg	124mg	3.2mg	0.38mg	0.28mg
Pecan	667	8%	18%	67%	5%	36mg	291mg	128mg	2.0mg	0.29mg	0.19mg
Pine nut	568	12%	19%	61%	6%	8mg	35mg	0	0	0.43mg	0.21mg
Coconut	354	3%	15%	33%	46%	14mg	113mg	0	3.0mg	0.15mg	0.06mg
Peanut	567	26%	16%	49%	7%	58mg	383mg	0	0	1.00mg	0.27mg
Acrocomia palm	n/a	13%	7%	67%	4%	0.1mg	0.1mg	0	0	0	0
FOR COMPARISON											
Sunflower seed	570	23%	19%	50%	5%	116mg	705mg	59mg	0	0.94mg	0.50mg

ABBREVIATIONS

Cal: Calories   Prot: Protein   Carbo: Carbohydrates

Ca: Calcium   Lys: Lysine   Meth: Methionine

Phos: Phosphorus

TYPES OF FAT	CONTAINED IN
Polyunsaturated: the fat less likely to be converted into cholesterol in the body.	Almonds, walnuts, etc.
Monounsaturated: fat found in vegetable oils.	Almonds, walnuts, etc.
Saturated: fat often found in meats and other animal products.	Brazils, macadamias, fresh coconuts, palm fruits

FRUITS AND BERRIES

Fruits and berries are consumed by nearly all parrots in the wild. However, those available commercially vary in their food value. Because fruit is mainly water and has no fat content (except for banana), you can offer as much of it as your parrot wants. Unlike sunflower seed, for example, which is attractive for its high fat content, a parrot will not consume too much fruit.

Fruit analysis

Below is an analysis of various fruits, showing their approximate Vitamin A content:

Mg per 100 g

Apricot	1,380*
Tomato	600*
Peach	535
Orange	205
Blackberry	165
Grapes	100
Banana	81
Apple	44
Melon (honeydew)	40
Pear	20

* expressed in terms of beta-carotene

Some species need more fruit than others. Parrots should be encouraged to take those that are high in Vitamin A, such as tomatoes and apricots. Apricots also contain essential trace elements—iron, copper, and phosphorus—and, in their dried form, contain more protein than any other dried fruit.

Vitamin A is crucially important in maintaining tissue lining and keeping the respiratory, digestive, and urinary tracts in good condition.

Other suitable fruits are papaya, mango, guava, kiwi, and cactus, and seasonal soft fruits such as red currants, blueberries, raspberries, and cranberries. It is not a good idea to offer blackberries, elderberries, and other fruits that stain heavily to parrots kept indoors!

These soft berries (also hawthorn berries) can be frozen for use throughout the year. It does not matter that the flesh of the fruit is somewhat soggy after freezing as parrots are only interested in the pips (seeds). It is the seeds in kiwi, cactus, and guava that attract some parrots. Oranges should be offered with the skin intact, in small pieces. It is likely to be ignored unless the orange is sweet. Juicy tangerines are a favorite with many parrots.

Pomegranates

Pomegranates are among the healthiest fruits available. They are loaded with Vitamin B2 (riboflavin) and contain manganese (2 mg per 100 g), an essential trace element. Parrots love the

translucent red seeds. If a pomegranate is cut open when the
interior is still whitish, the parrots will ignore the fruit. You
should cut pomegranates into pieces, leaving their skin
intact. To extend their season, consider buying a number
of cases; wrap each fruit individually in newspaper, and
store it in a cool place.

Bananas

Bananas are an excellent food. One fresh banana is said to contain as much as 185 mg of potassium, 16 mg of magnesium,
13 mg of phosphorus, 135 mg of chlorine, 60 mg of
sulfur, 4 mg of calcium, traces of iodine and bromine,
and 95 IU of Vitamin A. A few slices of banana daily
will supplement your parrot's diet with elements that
may be lacking from many other food items. You need
to learn the degree of ripeness that appeals to each individual bird. Cut the banana across (in round sections)
and offer it in the skin.

Stone fruits

You can offer stone fruits such as peaches and plums,
but your parrot might refuse them. Apricots are the most
beneficial. It is important to wash most fruits before you
feed them to your parrot, as they might have been
sprayed with harmful chemicals. Fruits such as apples
should be crisp, and grapes and pears should be
firm, not overripe.

Avoid a mixture of soft fruits as these end up as a
sludgy mixture that will ferment in hot weather and
attract insects. Choose with care the fruits that you
place in the same container. It is better to feed two fruits

two to three times a day rather than mix them all and offer them at one feed. Fruit should be offered in small quantities that will be eaten within a couple of hours. If they remain a long time in the dish they lose their appeal. Offer fruit in a stainless steel container, separate from dry food items.

For added enjoyment, you can hang whole or half fruits on a stainless steel holder (obtainable from pet stores). If your bird refuses to eat certain fruits and vegetables, it may sample them if you disguise them as playthings rather than food items. You could, for example, hang a pair of cherries on a toy or a swing.

Dried fruits

Dried fruits such as sultanas and raisins are rich in potassium and iron, and parrots relish them after they have been soaked in water for a few hours until soft and plump. Dried figs contain tiny, crunchy seeds that are rich in minerals; you can offer the figs dry.

Left: *Your parrot's fresh-fruit intake is essential to its health and well-being.*

VEGETABLES

Some parrots do not eat fresh vegetables with the same enthusiasm as fruit. You could encourage them to try by hanging the vegetables on a steel fruit holder (made for parrots) or attaching them to a toy. Many parrots will ignore vegetables if the food dish is full of seed, so greatly reduce the amount of seed in the morning. If the parrots refuse the vegetables (and/or fruit), try putting a stick of celery through the bars, or try cooking carrot, red bell pepper, and broccoli and mixing it, cut into small pieces, with a favorite food.

Vegetable offerings can include sugar snap or snow peas, young, tender peas in the pod, raw or par-boiled carrots, green beans, chopped zucchini, and celery, as well as red bell peppers and their seeds. Red bell peppers are more beneficial than green or yellow ones because they contain more beta-carotene, the precursor to Vitamin A. Another idea is to make use of sweet potatoes and yams. Parrots also relish frozen or thawed peas and corn. Light yellow, soft, and tender fresh corn is a great favorite. You should offer it raw in small pieces. Older corn is hard and parrots are more likely to accept it after it has been lightly cooked or frozen. Note that most kinds of avocado are poisonous to parrots.

Vegetable mash

For recently weaned young, it is worth making a mash of various items. Ingredients can include a pack of mixed frozen vegetables (carrots, peas, corn) and a few soaked or cooked legumes added to hard-boiled egg, carrot, and whole-wheat bread that have been blended in a food processor. Chopped walnuts sprinkled on top will encourage macaws to sample this food.

Left and below: *Carrots, broccoli, red bell peppers, and dark-green leaves are valuable for their beta-carotene content.*

WILD FOODS

Many parrot owners appear to be unaware of the benefits of feeding what they would describe as weeds. Such plants are the natural foods of many parakeets and other parrots. The leaves and roots of sowthistle (*Sonchus*) and dandelion (*Taraxacum officinale*) contain much Vitamin A and the flowers are full of pollen.

Dandelion is a very common weed, with long leaves, usually jagged, that rise upward in a tight cluster, or rosette. Some types have leaves that are less jagged. The leaves are shiny and without hairs. It has a thick, dark brown root, white and milky inside. The flowers are familiar, and comprise a golden yellow crown on a straight stem. The medicinal effects of this plant have been known for centuries. Dandelion contains more beta-carotene, ounce for ounce, than carrot, which helps to maintain a parrot's red plumage and assists in repairing liver and kidney damage. It is said to be a good source of calcium. The younger the leaf, the richer it is in food and dietetic value. It is harder to digest the older leaves. Minerals found in dandelion (and lacking in dry seeds) are sodium, iron, and manganese.

Sowthistle

Sowthistle also has yellow flowers. The best is the smooth type (Sonchus oleraceus) as parrots do not like to eat the leaves of the prickly species (Sonchus asper).

Chickweed

Chickweed (Stellaria media) is a great favorite with parakeets. Most gardens, unless zealously weeded, have chickweed, sowthistle, or dandelion growing somewhere. You can maintain small patches of chickweed by watering them and keeping them free of other weeds. Most people can find a nearby area with beneficial weeds that are not likely to have been contaminated with pesticides, but also be aware of possible lead contamination from passing cars.

Dock

An almost universally popular plant is dock in its seeding form. The two types of dock commonly seen are curled dock (Rumex crispus) and broad-leaved dock (Rumex obtusifolio), with leaves that are waxy, but not curled edges. Some parrots like dock green, whereas others prefer it when the seeds are ripe and red-brown. Look for dock near clumps of stinging nettles. The two are often found together, so it is a good idea to wear gloves when collecting dock! I simply cut the stems off near the base with pruning shears and put the stem around the cage bars. Many seed-eating parrots are passionately fond of seeding dock.

LEGUMES

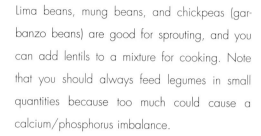

This is the term given to dried peas, beans, and lentils. They should be soaked, drained, and washed, then left in a warm place for a few hours until they have just started to sprout. They are then a good source of protein and vitamins. The food value is reduced if they are cooked but they become more palatable. Legumes provide protein and vary the diet in a healthy manner. You can introduce young macaws, Amazons, *Pionus*, and Grays, for example, to cooked legumes at the weaning stage before introducing them to seed. They will enjoy warm, soft foods and will be more likely to accept a varied diet in later life. Some bird-food companies sell legume mixtures for sprouting or cooking. Be aware that some kinds of beans are not popular with parrots and they may ignore them, and that red kidney beans are said to contain toxic substances unless cooked.

Lima beans, mung beans, and chickpeas (garbanzo beans) are good for sprouting, and you can add lentils to a mixture for cooking. Note that you should always feed legumes in small quantities because too much could cause a calcium/phosphorus imbalance.

HUMAN FOODS

Some of our own food items can make a useful addition to the diet: cubes of hard cheese that contain a small amount of calcium, hard-boiled egg, lean ham, chicken, and cooked lentils for their protein component. Cooked vegetables might find more favor than raw ones. Even after cooking, carrots, spinach, tomatoes, and red bell peppers are valuable sources of Vitamin A, as are cooked apricots. Baked beans are also suitable for their protein and Vitamin A content.

Chicken and turkey carcasses are an excellent source of protein and calcium and provide beak occupation for macaws, Amazons, and cockatoos. You only need to remove the small sharp bones. Middle bones of lamb are also good. A friend, whose elderly Gray Parrot ignores most fruit, boils an egg, cuts it up into small pieces, including the shell, and mixes it with seed. Both whole-wheat and whole-grain bread are popular, especially when toasted.

Foods to avoid are those high in fat, salt, and sugar, such as chips, salted peanuts, and cookies. Avoid offering chocolate, especially good-quality chocolate, and most varieties of avocado, as they are poisonous to parrots.

GRIT AND TRACE MINERALS

Seed-eating parrots need grit in the gizzard to grind up hard foods. Parrots not offered grit are likely to destroy woodwork and bricks instead. Bird-food manufacturers package and offer diff-erent kinds of grit. Mineral grit consists of a variety of small stones such as lime-stone and oyster shell, which comprise calcium carbonate, quartz, and charcoal (soluble). Acids in the pro-ventriculus (the first part of a bird's stomach, where digestive enzymes act upon the food before it goes to the gizzard) digest calcium carbon-ate, and therefore the calcium carbonate is of no use in grinding down food, but is a good source of calcium.

An effective source of calcium is particularly important to a laying female. Calcium should be available to laying females in three forms: grit, cuttlefish bone, and a calcium supplement containing Vitamin D. The latter is of vital impor-tance to your parrot's health.

A typical grit product contains several kinds of stone, of which the bird might select the kind it needs and leave the rest. Thus you should completely empty and refill the grit container at intervals.

Vets believe that grit can be highly beneficial to a bird that has a problem digesting its food or that has a pancreatic dysfunction. Grit improves the surface area on which the digestive enzymes act. (Enzymes cannot function properly if the diet is deficient in certain minerals or trace elements.) Birds need minute prop-ortions of the following trace elements found in bird grit and powdered mineral supplements: zinc, iron, iodine, manganese, sulfur, selenium, cobalt, and molybdenum. If you mainly feed your birds seed and do not give them access to fresh soil or green plants with roots and soil, or give them mineral supplements, they will be deficient in trace elements. Other major elements also found in grit include calcium, phosphorus, sodium, and chlorine. Sodium, for example, assists digestion, and chlorine is said to help prevent excessive deposition of fat.

Above: *A typical grit mixture.*

8

Health and beauty

There are four golden rules for maintaining good health in a companion parrot over the long term, namely maintaining a balanced diet, preventing stressful situations, avoiding exposure to or contact with diseased birds or recently imported wild-caught parrots, and keeping the cage and environment clean.

The metabolism of birds is very rapid, especially in small species, thus early detection of poor health is vital. The condition of a sick bird deteriorates much more rapidly than that of a dog, for example. Parrot owners should always be aware of subtle changes in normal behavior, such as a bird sleeping for longer periods, becoming quieter, or eating less. A change in the color or the consistency of the droppings without a change in diet (offering foods such as pomegranate or beets, for example, which obviously affect the color) is another possible sign of poor health. Droppings in which the urine (the white part) is tinged with yellow indicates a kidney problem. The eyes of a sick parrot will appear dull, or even sunken, and will be closed for long periods. Or a parrot may blink a lot, as though trying not to close its eyes in your presence.

Opposite: *The bright eye and alert expression indicate that this macaw is healthy.*

Do not delay in contacting a vet, preferably an avian vet. You should try to locate one in advance of acquiring your parrot. If you can find a vet who understands the treatment of parrots, take yours for an annual checkup. You might also consider taking out veterinary insurance, as treatment can be expensive.

A sick bird has two vital requirements: warmth and fluid. Every bird owner should have a dull-emitter (heat, no light) infrared lamp with a holder and reflector. You can purchase one from a specialist bird or poultry supplier. You should place the lamp above one end or at the side of the sick bird's cage so that it can move away from the heat if it so desires. Hospital cages are not recommended because the temperature is constant throughout (the bird cannot move away from the heat) and the interior lacks humidity. In an emergency you might supply heat by placing the cage beside a radiator and putting a towel over it to help retain the heat.

Sick birds fail to eat and drink enough. Many die from dehydration rather than from not eating. A vet can give fluids by various means, and this is why it is so important to consult a vet if a parrot ceases to feed.

Left: *An infrared lamp that emits only heat is the best heat source for a sick bird.*

GOOD HYGIENE

Cleanliness and good ventilation are vital when keeping birds in the home. With the proliferation of serious and fatal avian viral diseases in recent years, this is more important than ever. In an enclosed environment, viral particles spread easily from one cage to the next.

Few disinfectants are effective against viruses. One exception is Virkon S (manufactured by Antec International, a division of DuPont). It also works well against bacteria, molds, and fungi. You can use it indoors for cleaning down walls and cages and you can even use it to sterilize water. I recommend Ark-Klens from Vetark Professional for use against psittacosis (chlamydia). The same company produces an iodophore disinfectant that is effective against viruses, and fungi such as aspergillus. If you need to handle a sick bird, use a hand disinfectant and a hand scrub afterward.

You must keep perches clean, as dirty ones are a major source of infection of the feet and eyes. Cleanliness in all areas is essential if you are to maintain a sense of pride in your birds.

Right: *Ensure that the cage, toys, and perches are all kept clean.*

OBESITY

Many captive parrots become overweight because of an incorrect diet and/or a lack of exercise due to wing clipping. Obesity can also result if you offer your parrot a diet so deficient in nutrients that it overeats in an attempt to correct this deficiency. Boredom might also cause obesity; the parrot has nothing to do, so it eats—rather like comfort eating in humans.

Limit high-fat foods such as sunflower seeds and do not offer human foods with a high-fat content such as chips and crackers. The need for fats and oils in a particular species varies according to the diet it would consume in its natural environment. The species most likely to become obese when incorrectly fed include white cockatoos, Galahs (Roseate Cockatoos), Eclectus, Budgerigars, Amazons, and *Pionus*.

What can be done to reduce the weight of an obese parrot? Obviously you need to correct the diet. Most overweight parrots consume too many sunflower seeds. Either you should convert to pellets or limit your offering of sunflower seeds. To do this, offer only a few grains in the morning, plus fruit, vegetables, and/or legumes. Parrots are at their hungriest in the morning, so even if they do not consume much at first, eventually they should do so. In the afternoon offer a little more seed. You should reduce the daily intake of sunflower seeds by half. If you have more than one parrot, place the overweight bird's cage near one that consumes a good variety of items, as this will encourage it to try a wider variety of foods. Legumes are good for their high protein value.

Right: *Budgerigars are prone to obesity. They should be full-winged and exercise outside the cage.*

Your parrot may be overeating because it has a serious protein deficiency, which is very likely if you are only feeding it seeds. Protein is essential to replace body tissues and feathers.

Exercise is very important. If your parrot is wing-clipped, its opportunities for exercise are limited. Twice daily take the parrot on your hand and move your hand up and down so the bird is forced to flap its wings. At first it might breathe heavily at this exertion, so do not overdo it, but continue this exercise until either it is full-winged or has lost weight. If diet and lack of exercise are not the reason for obesity in your parrot, you should consult an avian vet. There could be a serious health problem, such as kidney disease.

CALCIUM DEFICIENCY

Gray Parrots are more susceptible than other parrots to hypocalcemia (calcium deficiency). It causes seizures and eventually death if it is left untreated. I suspect that few Gray Parrots that feed mainly on seed without a calcium supplement live beyond their teens. Lack of exposure to ultraviolet light is believed to play a part in this syndrome and also affects the level of the parathyroid hormone in the body.

Two heartbreaking phone calls that I received one evening described a scenario that is sadly so common. The Gray, a wild-caught bird, much-loved, and with the family for 17 years, had been "staggering around his cage" and then fell onto the floor. He managed to climb up the cage but could not perch; he clung to the side with his beak. I advised the owners to get the bird to a vet as a matter of life or death. It was evening, so it took about an hour to find one who could see their parrot. Another phone call relayed the sad story. It was too late. He died as the calcium injection was given. This Gray had been seen by an avian vet a few months previously. At the time he had received a calcium injection and the owners were advised to put a liquid calcium supplement in the drinking water. This supplement is like a syrup; it is heavier than water and therefore drops to the bottom of the container. As Grays drink little, the chances of him ingesting any of the calcium were remote. His diet consisted almost entirely of sunflower seed and peanuts.

The whole family were in tears when he died. He had accompanied them everywhere. His owner would even phone him when the family went on vacation and her mother was looking after him, and he became very excited on hearing her voice. Through her tears, his owner told me: "After he died I cuddled him. It was the only time I was ever able to hold him." A wild-caught bird, he truly was a member of the family and could have lived out his potential lifespan if only his family had been better informed on health matters. It is very sad to hear the same story so often.

HEAVY-METAL POISONING

Ingestion of zinc causes degeneration of the liver and kidneys, and will eventually result in death if untreated. Zinc is found in such objects as keys, some coins, nails, staples, padlocks, zippers, and some kinds of paint (especially anti-rust paint). Some kinds of D clips (for hanging toys) contain zinc, so use only stainless steel items. Mercury is also highly toxic. It can be found on the backs of old mirrors.

Window screens are usually only dangerous if they have been badly galvanized, leaving flakes of zinc on the wire that a parrot can ingest. It is often recommended to wipe the screens with vinegar and brush them thoroughly with a wire brush. While this might be effective in some cases, this treatment (carried out vigorously) did not prevent the loss of one of my lorikeets, despite immediate treatment. This is probably because lories and lorikeets, unlike other parrots, actively lick items. If in doubt about galvanized wire, you can get it powder-coated, with a request that the coating does not contain zinc. This finish is quite hardwearing, but larger parrots can bite it off. Modern cages are less likely to contain zinc in their finishes as the problem is now well understood. However, do not buy cheap, imported, welded screen as it is likely to be dangerous.

Right and above: *Parrots like to play with spoons, zippers, and keys—these must be stainless steel.*

TOXIC PLANTS

Avoid keeping certain houseplants that are known to be toxic to parrots. These include the castor bean (*Ricinus communis*), which contains ricin—a highly poisonous substance; dieffenbachia, grown for its foliage; the Swiss cheese plant (*Monstera deliciosa*); amaryllis, and related plants such as daffodils and ivy (*Hedera helix*). A highly poisonous species—not known as a house-plant, but commonly planted in the tropics—is the shrub oleander (*Nerium oleander*). Lantana is also poisonous. Also look out for pelleted fertilizers that might be in the soil of a newly pur-chased plant, as these might be toxic.

DISEASES
Viral diseases

One of the most serious viral diseases is proventricular dilatation disease (PDD), known as macaw wasting disease when first described. Gray Parrots and macaws are among the parrot species most likely to be affected. Failure to gain weight, or unexplained weight loss, prolonged juvenile behavior, a lack of coordination, and undigested seeds in droppings are all subtle signs. Food passes slowly through the intestines, but this also applies to birds affected by other diseases. There is no reliable diagnostic test in living birds. A negative result from a biopsy test is not conclu-sive because it is such a complex disease with many different symptoms. Radiographs and crop biopsies can be performed to try to determine if the disease is present. The probable cause is a virus that attacks the nervous system. It results in lesions of the nerves that sup-ply the muscles of the gastrointestinal tract (including the crop) and/or the central nervous system. A vet can

Left: *Do not allow parrots to bite at amaryllis plants.*

attempt diagnosis by biopsy, taking a small piece of the wall of the crop. Taking a biopsy from other parts of the gut is possible but too dangerous and could cause death. Only a few parrots have been known to recover from this disease.

The other common disease, psittacine beak and feather disease (PBFD), is caused by a circovirus. As already mentioned, parrots sold to pet stores at an early age are susceptible because many such stores offer Budgerigars—a significant proportion of which are affected by PBFD. The virus enters a gland near the cloaca

Anatomy of a parrot

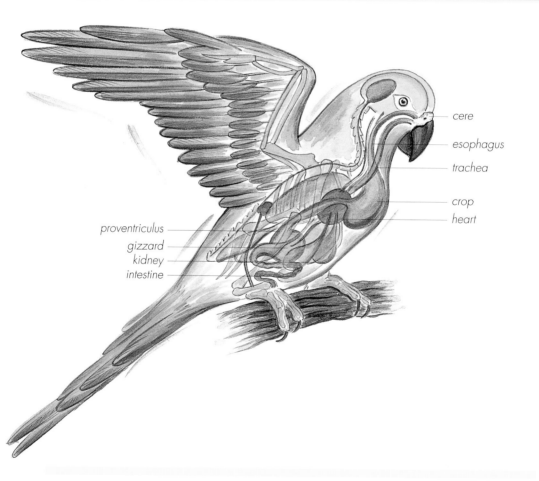

cere
esophagus
trachea
crop
heart
proventriculus
gizzard
kidney
intestine

known as the bursa of Fabricius. The bursa disappears in a few weeks or months when the bird's immune system is stronger. Some birds recover spontaneously, while others are so seriously affected that they eventually die from secondary infections.

British avian vet and parrot breeder Nigel Harcourt-Brown informed me that the virus invades the germinal cells of growing feathers and the beak, as well as the bone marrow. It kills many of the cells and initially prevents the formation of powder down, causing malformed feathers, feather loss, or dirty feathers in white cockatoos. The germinal feather cells are injured and fail to produce melanin, thus producing some abnormally colored feathers. In the next stage of the disease the erupting feathers stop growing and fall out. In African species, such as Grays and Senegals, the bone marrow is severly affected. The white blood cell count falls dramatically and finally the bird becomes anemic.

ASPERGILLOSIS

This is commonly found in newly imported parrots, due to the bad conditions in which they have been kept, a diet deficient in Vitamin A, and stress. A common fungal respiratory infection, it is usually fatal. The cause is the fungus *Aspergillus fumigatus*, which might be found anywhere, but is especially common on moldy food or other vegetable matter, including hay. It can be found on decaying food on a damp cage floor, damp nesting material, seeds or peanuts stored in a damp place, or on wood shavings. Shavings or wood chips sold in bales as bedding for horses with stable allergies or lung disease should be safe.

Symptoms of aspergillosis are wheezy breathing and shortage of breath at times of stress or exertion. By the time this occurs, the disease has generally progressed too far for treatment to be effective because the air sacs or the lungs have become filled with the fungus. Affected birds will lose weight. If the disease affects the syrinx (the voice box), loss of voice might occur. Treatment might be successful if diagnosis occurs at an early stage. Nebulization at a vet's clinic offers hope of a cure if the condition is not too well established. Prevention is very important.

INJURIES

Normally one should use only ointments prescribed by a vet, as some ointments are absorbed through the skin and this could prove to be poisonous. I prefer the use of natural soothing remedies such as aloe vera gel. For example, when one of my lorikeets injured the skin on her back, I cleaned it with witch hazel and then used the gel. The bleeding stopped and she did not bite herself again. In another instance, my Amazon injured her eyelid on a piece of cuttlefish bone. The eyelid became enormously swollen. A vet prescribed viscous fusidic acid eye drops. I had to discontinue their use because the eye did not absorb the drops well, therefore my Amazon rubbed her eye on her scapulars, leaving a greasy patch on the plumage (after only three applications). This

greasy patch irritated her as much as the eye. In other circumstances, a bird might have rubbed its eye on the perch, with the risk of reinfection. In the past I have used dibromopropamidine isethionate BP for an eye infection in a small parrot with excellent results and no problems.

BEAUTY
Plumage care

Many parrots crave water on their plumage. Others do not like being sprayed and they object or fly off at the sight of the sprayer because they do not like to get wet. However, some parrots that behave like this enjoy bathing in a large shallow dish, and you can encourage them by placing a green leaf (such as lettuce) in the dish. If this is not successful, you could buy a pump-action spray with a nozzle that produces a fine mist, which may be more acceptable.

It is important for your parrot's health, and that of family members, to minimize the quantity of airborne white powder-down that your parrot produces. You can do this by ensuring that it regularly

has water on its plumage. Spraying has extra benefits for clipped birds as it stimulates them to flap their wings vigorously. This can be a great source of enjoyment.

Many parrots enjoy showering with their owners, provided that the water is not too hot. Do not expect most parrots to keep their plumage perfect without your help. The home environment is too dry for this to be possible.

Above: *A parrot, such as this Quaker Parakeet, spends long periods every day preening its plumage.*

Left: *Regular access to water will ensure your parrot's plumage is maintained in good condition. This macaw loves to be showered in the bath.*

MOLTING

All family members make a degree of mess that annoys the house-proud, and this is equally true of parrots. When they are molting, their white down feathers seem to get everywhere. Under normal circumstances parrots molt once a year or, occasionally, twice a year, but birds kept under artificial light for long periods might molt more often.

When a parrot is molting, this should be apparent only by the feathers on the cage floor; in other words, the plumage should look normal. Beware the vendor who states of a bird with large bald areas that it is molting. This is untrue. Either it is plucking itself or it has a viral disease that causes loss of plumage.

In many species the molt is protracted and almost imperceptible in the small number of feathers lost simultaneously. In a single parrot the clue that a bird is starting to molt will be the unopened feather sheaths on the head—the only area that it cannot reach to preen. If these sheaths are hard and do not break off after a couple of weeks, spray the parrot daily with warm water from a plant mister and/or keep it in an area of higher humidity. You might even need to install a humidifier in the room.

In some parrots the molt is more rapid and obvious when you look on the cage floor, yet at no time are missing feathers apparent. Molting birds might have a couple of growing primary or secondary wing feathers that are shorter than the others, but a healthy bird will never be missing more than a couple of full-grown flight feathers. The new one pushes out the previous feather in that follicle. The growing feather is known as a blood quill because the core of the quill is filled with blood. The blood supply sustains the rapid growth of the feather; when growth is complete the blood supply is sealed off. Damage to a blood feather can result in bleeding, with the amount of blood lost appearing to be dramatic. A vet should remove the quill if bleeding is severe.

Regrowth

Most feathers are replaced annually, although within a period of 12 months some of the primary wing feathers might not be molted. Exceptions occur in the case of a "shock molt." If a parrot has a sudden frightening experience (perhaps being caught with a net), it could instantly shed some wing and/or tail feathers. This is a defense mechanism whereby a predator that would try to catch it in the wild might end up with a mouthful of feathers and the bird would escape. Avoid stressful events, such as moving the bird to a new location, during the molt.

Parrots that have suffered from malnutrition might not molt for a long time. Molting birds need adequate quantities of food, and certain levels of protein and calcium. A food shortage for even a couple of days can result in defective feathers. This is also apparent in young

Left: *A humidifier might solve the problem of dry plumage.*

parrots in the nest, in which most of the primaries and secondaries are growing simultaneously. If the chick is deprived of food or suffers from stress or disease, the feathers will grow with a dark line across them. These are called stress marks.

Experiments with poultry have shown that when the diet contained only 3 percent protein, molting did not occur. When protein levels were increased to 5 percent molting commenced. The exact requirements of parrots are unknown and probably differ according to the species, but the message is clear: supplement the protein content of your parrot's diet as soon as it starts to molt. You can give your parrot cooked lean meat such as chicken (but not the sharp bones), hard-boiled egg, cubes of cheese, and even cooked legumes and lentils. For smaller species, a good-quality egg-rearing food made for parrots or parakeets is suitable.

Young parrots molt at between about 5 and 11 months according to the species, although in small species such as parrotlets the molt might commence at 4 months. The head feathers are usually the first to be lost, but during the first molt the wing and tail feathers are not shed. A parrot might be slightly irritable during the molt. If it does not want to come out of its cage, leave it in peace.

Feather types

FLIGHT FEATHER

Parrots have 10 flight feathers, also known as primaries, in each wing.

TAIL FEATHER

Parrots have 12 tail feathers.

DOWN FEATHER

Down feathers insulate the plumage.

CARE OF NAILS AND BEAK

A regular supply of fresh-cut branches will help to keep a parrot's beak and nails in good condition. A healthy parrot kept well should not need to have its nails or beak trimmed. My Amazon parrot is over 40 years old and her beak is in perfect condition. I attribute this to the fact that she daily spends an hour or more crunching wood. An overgrown upper mandible might be caused by long-term lack of gnawing material, by a dietary deficiency, or as the result of a previous beak injury.

An avian vet or a trusted vet who is used to handling parrots can use a dental hand piece or a rotating mini-tool to trim the beak. It often helps to place a piece of wood, such as a hard dowel, between the parrot's mandibles so that it can bite on this. After trimming, the vet must shape the beak or it will look unsightly and the parrot might find it difficult to feed.

It is not uncommon for the upper mandible to become overgrown in aged parrots—and this is often associated with liver disease.

Note that the upper mandible contains a vein and a nerve that reach almost to the tip. If the

Left: *This young macaw does not need to have its nails trimmed.*

vein is ruptured blood will flow and, without the use of a cauterizer, it can be difficult to stop the bleeding. One can try holding talcum powder or flour against it to help clotting. If the tip of a parrot's beak is broken off there might be no bleeding, but the parrot can appear very ill because the nerve is exposed. This is very painful, so the parrot will not want to eat. It must be given soft foods, and subcutaneous fluids if necessary.

If a nail is broken, resulting in blood loss, it is advisable to remove the perches in the cage, making the parrot cling to the bars or the wire; it is then less likely that the parrot will wipe the blood clot off the tip of the nail.

Do not allow the nails to become overgrown unless a parrot is old. If you have a young parrot with sharp nails, do not cut them. Gently file them with an emery board. If trimming the nails is necessary you must take great care not to cut into the

Nail clipping

Nails should be clipped only if they are very long. Note position of the vein (if possible)

and cut well below it. If the vein cannot be seen, cut only a small length of the nail.

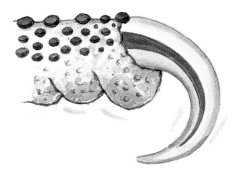 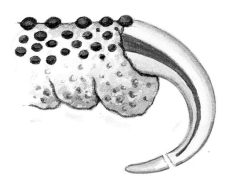

vein. You can see the vein in a bird with light nails ,but not if the nails are dark. Unqualified or inexperienced people have caused parrots painful injury and serious blood loss by cutting into the vein.

In an older bird, especially one with arthritis, longer nails help the bird to balance and grip the perch. Only trim them if they are dangerously overgrown. Two people can carry out this procedure. One holds the parrot in a towel to restrain the head, and the other holds the foot firmly in one hand and trims the nails with the other hand. You can use human nail clippers or bird nail clippers. As it is usually difficult to see where the vein ends, clipping a bit at a time means that the worst that can happen is that you cut the tip of the vein, with minimal bleeding or discomfort.

Above: *An emery board can be used to gently file the sharp nails of a young parrot. Human nail clippers, or nail scissors designed for birds, can be used to trim the nails of older parrots.*

OLD AGE

Signs of aging in parrots are similar to those in humans. They include arthritis and joint stiffness, deteriorating eyesight, cataracts and other eye disorders, changes in the iris color, and loss of tone in the eyelids. The plumage might become dull and lusterless in very old parrots, but should maintain its condition well if you spray the parrot three times a week. Sometimes there might be a change in plumage color. Thinning of the skin and depigmentation on the feet are other signs of old age.

To counteract these changes, the diet should be excellent and should include plenty of fresh foods containing antioxidants, such as tomatoes. Keep processed food to a minimum. Reputable bottled mineral water is recommended, as tap water contains chemicals that can be harmful. My Amazon, who is at least 40 years old, suffers from arthritis in her legs and wings. The only water I offer her is a certain brand of sparkling spring water that comes from a spring notable for its beneficial waters and highly recommended for human arthritis sufferers. For a short time, my local supermarket was temporarily out of stock of this particular brand of bottled water, and within a couple of weeks my Amazon had started to fall off her perch. Failing to grip the perch well or falling off is a symptom of arthritis.

Opposite: *The nails of a parrot with arthritis can be maintained in a longer condition than normal to help it grip the perch.*
Right: *At 40-plus years, the author's Amazon is in excellent feather condition due to frequent spraying.*

9

Rehoming your parrot

It is a sad fact that few parrots spend their entire lives with the same family unless they die young. To successfully rehome a parrot is difficult. If the situation arises where you must do this, think about the options very carefully. Do not act on the spur of the moment.

If a new home is sought for a parrot because it has behavioral problems, I would strongly advise the owner to try to correct these problems, perhaps with the help of another experienced parrot owner. In many instances all that is needed is some kind discipline and a little training. It is amazing how different a parrot can become after it has been taught to "Step up" (see page 122) and given more focused attention.

I would emphasize that it is not easy to rehome an adult parrot. Even as I was writing this chapter, a lady contacted me and described circumstances that perfectly illustrated this. Her 11-year-old Lesser Sulfur-crested Cockatoo male had been her husband's bird and was very tame. Sadly her husband had died a few months previously. Although she liked the cockatoo she admitted that she was "a bit afraid of him" and could only handle him by persuading him to step onto a broom handle. He was housed in a cage on casters and she always moved him into whichever room she was using, as he became very noisy if he could not see her.

Opposite: *If you need to find a new home for your parrot, remember that its future happiness depends on the new owner's capacity to meet its physical and emotional needs.*

Opposite: *These unwanted parrots are fortunate to be homed by a keeper who allows them to take daily flights.*
Below: *Aviary birds, such as Quaker Parakeets, may be easier to rehome than pet parrots.*

Some friends had expressed a great interest and took him into their home. They kept him in their greenhouse. However, after one week they brought him back. He wanted to be where they were, not confined to the greenhouse, so he screamed repeatedly for attention.

When you keep a highly intelligent creature like a cockatoo, it is, as the lady commented, like having a small child. You cannot just put it in another room and expect it to amuse itself. So if you are rehoming a parrot, make sure that the people proposing to take it are aware of this. Also remember that many parrots have a strong preference for either male or female human company. To send them to a new home that lacks the favored sex is a recipe for failure.

GUIDELINES TO REHOMING

First of all, do not give your parrot away unless it is to a close friend who knows it. Many people do not value something they have not paid for. In addition, there is the temptation to sell a free parrot to make money. One way to try to find a suitable home is to place a classified advertisement in a specialist parrot magazine or a general birdkeeping publication.

Advertisements in local and free newspapers often attract people who do not read parrot magazines and have little knowledge.

You might also contact the secretary of your local parrot club (if one exists). The person who

runs the group might be able to suggest a suitable member who can help. If your parrot is one of the less common species he or she might be able to put you in touch with someone who has contacts regarding this type of parrot.

If you advertise your parrot and receive several replies, how can you judge which person might give your parrot the best home? If the caller's first question is, "Does it talk?" cross him or her off the list. Anyone who wants a parrot only for its ability to mimic is not the right kind of owner. Ask the caller a few questions. Has he or she kept a parrot before? Why does she or he want to buy a parrot of that species? Are there any young children in the household? Who is at home during the day? You do not want your parrot to spend hours on its own. If the parrot is noisy, be honest about this so that you can assess the reaction. After talking to the person for two or three minutes you should have a good feel for how sensitive he or she is to the needs of a parrot. If you are not satisfied, but you do not want to offend, say that you have had several inquiries and you will let them know. Do not be pressured. The future of your parrot is at stake. If you feel the person or family might be suitable, ask if you can go and see them in their home. The environment and the family members are also important.

Parrot sanctuary

If you cannot find a suitable individual, should you consider a parrot sanctuary? This is a difficult question to answer: there are good and bad sanctuaries. However, a quick way to assess one is by the standard of accommodation. If the parrots are housed in individual cages in someone's house or building and there are many of them, their quality of life is unlikely to be good. How can they receive enough attention in these circumstances? Some well-meaning people take on an increasing number of birds, with the result that they do not care for them properly and the birds end up being worse off than in their previous situation.

On the other hand, there are a few sanctuaries where birds are housed in large outdoor flights with other members of their species and the quality of their lives is greatly improved. Once again, however, you must consider that a tame bird might be miserable away from people. Certain birds are not suited to this type of life:

they crave a close human relationship. Other tame birds will adapt. Not everyone can assess the potential of their parrot.

Rehoming organizations

Rehoming organizations operate in a different way from sanctuaries, taking in unwanted parrots, assessing them, and then trying to find a new permanent home for them. This makes sense because there is a limit to the number of birds that any sanctuary can take and often it reaches its limit very soon. The problem is that usually there are more par-

rots to be rehomed than there are suitable care-givers, so some might go out to unsuitable people.

Zoos

Many people who have contacted me about rehoming their parrot ask about donating them to zoos. However, zoos no longer accept parrots because they are offered so many. A small bird park might accept them, but in a climate where the zoo-visiting season is short, it must be remembered that they will see few people during most months of the year. A tame parrot that has been used to a lot of company will probably not be happy in such an environment. On the other hand, a wild-caught parrot that is not tame and needs space more than anything could adjust very well to the larger aviaries found in such places.

Above: *Most zoos no longer accept donated parrots because so many are offered.*

Contacts

UNITED STATES

AMERICAN FEDERATION OF AVICULTURE
P.O. Box 7312
N. Kansas City, MO 64116
Tel: (816) 421-2473
Email: afaoffice@aol.com
www.afabirds.org

AVICULTURAL SOCIETY OF AMERICA
P.O. Box 5516
Riverside, CA 92517
Tel: (951) 780-4102
E-mail: hhanson@earthlink.net
www.asabirds.org

CANADA

AVICULTURAL ADVANCEMENT COUNCIL OF CANADA
P.O. Box 123
Chemainus, B.C., V0R 1K0
Tel: (250) 246-4803
E-mail: exec@aacc.ca
www.islandnet.com/~aacc/

PARROT ASSOCIATION OF CANADA
637316 St. Vincent Township
R.R. #1 Meaford, ON, N4L 1W5
E-mail: genus_amazona@hotmail.com
www.parrotscanada.org

Publications

UNITED STATES

BIRDTALK and BIRDS USA
P.O. Box 6050
Mission Viejo, CA 92690
Tel: (949) 855-8822
www.birdtalkmagazine.com

AVICULTURAL SOCIETY BULLETIN
P.O. Box 5516
Riverside, CA 92517
Tel: (626) 289-4400
E-mail: sdingle@earthlink.net
www.asabirds.org/publication.htm

CANADA

THE AVICULTURE JOURNAL
P.O. Box 123
Chemainus, BC, V0R 1K0
Tel: (250) 246-4803
E-mail: exec@aacc.ca
www.islandnet.com/~aacc/

ENGLAND

PARROTS MAGAZINE
Imax Ltd
12 Riverside Business Centre
Brighton Road
Shoreham-by-Sea, England
BN43 6RE
Tel: (+1273) 464777
E-mail: parrots@imaxweb.co.uk
www.parrotmag.com

Glossary

Aflatoxins: Any one of a group of toxic compounds produced by certain molds, especially *Aspergillus flavus*, that contaminate stored food supplies such as animal feed and peanuts.

Bursa: A sac or saclike body cavity containing a viscous lubricating fluid, located between a tendon and a bone or at points of friction between moving structures.

Cere: The fleshy area above a parrot's beak. This is visible in most parrots. Only in adult Budgerigars is it a means of identifying their sex (brown in a female, deep blue in a male).

Circovirus: A genus of the *Circoviridae* family that infects fowl, swine, and psittacine birds.

CITES: Convention on International Trade in Endangered Species of Wild Fauna and Flora.

Cloaca: The single opening (vent) for the excretory and reproductive system.

Follicle: The tiny cavity within the skin from which the feather grows.

Genus (pural: genera): A group of closely related species, all of which share the first part of the scientific name.

Giardia: A genus of flagellate protozoans inhabiting the intestines of various animals, including one that is associated with diarrhea in humans.

Ionize: To convert, or be converted, totally or partially into ions.

Lores: The area (feathered in most parrots) between the eye and the beak.

Lutino: A mutation (usually yellow) in which the bird's plumage is devoid of pigment and the eyes are pink or red.

Lysine: An essential amino acid obtained by the hydrolysis of proteins and required by the body for optimum growth.

Mandibles: The two parts of the beak, known as the upper and lower mandibles.

Metabolism: The interrelated series of chemical interactions taking place within living organisms that provide the energy and nutrients to sustain life.

Methionine: A sulfur-containing essential amino acid obtained from various proteins or prepared synthetically and used as a dietary supplement.

Molybdenum: An essential trace element in plant nutrition, used in fertilizers, dyes, enamels, and reagents.

Monounsaturated fat: Of or relating to an organic compound, especially an oil or fatty acid, containing only one double or triple bond per molecule. Foods that contain monounsaturated fatty acids may decrease the amount of LDL cholesterol in the blood of humans and include olive, peanut, canola, and avocado oils.

Nares: The nostrils.

Neotropical: In relation to parrot species, those from South and Central America and the islands of the Caribbean. This region is also known as the New World.

Old World: Europe, Asia, and Africa—that is, the parts of the world known to Europeans before Columbus voyaged to the Americas.

Pantothenic acid: A yellow oily acid, $C_9H_{17}NO_5$, belonging to and found widely in plant and animal tissues.

Pieds: A mutation in which the original plumage color is altered with patches of white or some other color.

Psittacine: Of or belonging to the family *Psittacidae*, which includes the parrots, macaws, and parakeets.

Psittacosis: An infectious disease of parrots and many other birds caused by the bacterium *Chlamydia psittaci*. It is communicable to humans, in whom it produces high fever, severe headache, and symptoms similar to pneumonia. Also called parrot fever.

Subspecies: A different race that is separate geographically from other populations of that species.

Index

Photographic credits

Copyright © rests with primary photographer Rosemary Low, and with the following photographers and/or their agents listed below.

Key to locations **a** = above; **b** = below; **l** = left; **r** = right; **c** = center

Front cover	www.imagesofafrica.co.za	43b	Pete Oxford/naturepl.com/	103	Digital Images Solutions
back cover	(from left to right)		Photo Access	104	Jean-Michel Labat/Ardea.com
	Nigel Dennis/NHPA	45a	Dennis Avon/Ardea.com	106	Brian Cushing/
	Digital Images Solutions	45b	Francois Gohier/Ardea.com		papiliophotos.com
	Nigel Dennis/NHPA	46b	Mirko Stelzner/NHPA	108	Tamlyn Beaumont-Thomas
	Photo Access	48	Dennis Avon/Ardea.com	111	Gallo Images/Gettyimages.com
	Ernie Janes/NHPA	50	Sue Graham Smith	112	Johann Theron
1	John Daniels/Ardea.com	51	Luiz C. Marigo/Still Pictures	117	John Daniels/Ardea.com
2	Donald Trounson/Ardea.com	52b	Dennis Avon/Ardea.com	119	www.imagesofafrica.co.za
4–5	www.imagesofafrica.co.za	53a	Dennis Avon/Ardea.com	120	Jean-Michel Labat/Ardea.com
6c	www.imagesofafrica.co.za	55a	Nigel Dennis/NHPA	130	Anipix/Panorama Publishers
9	Gallo Images/Gettyimages.com	55b	Adriadne Van Zandbergen/	132	Digital Images Solutions
10	UlrikeSchanze/naturepl.com/		www.imagesofafrica.co.za	135	John Daniels/Ardea.com
	Photo Access	56–57	www.imagesofafrica.co.za	137	Ernie Janes/NHPA
11	Mike Jackson/Still Pictures	60–61	Les Rance	140	Martin Harvey/NHPA
19	Ann & Steven Toon/NHPA	62	Dennis Avon/Ardea.com	142	www.imagesofafrica.co.za
20	Photo Access	63	Digital Images Solutions	143–145	Digital Images Solutions
22	Jean-Michel Labat/Ardea.com	65–66a	Digital Images Solutions	146	Digital Images Solutions
24	Johann Theron	69	www.imagesofafrica.co.za	147–149	www.imagesofafrica.co.za
26	Lynn M. Stone/naturepl.com/	71	www.imagesofafrica.co.za	152	www.imagesofafrica.co.za
	Photo Access	72	Ernie Janes/NHPA	154	www.imagesofafrica.co.za
27	Roland Seitre/Still Pictures	73	Michael Sewell/Still Pictures	155	Digital Images Solutions
30	Ernie Janes/NHPA	77	Anipix/Panorama Publishers	158	www.imagesofafrica.co.za
32	Gallo Images/Gettyimages.com	78	Stephen Dalton/NHPA	159	Digital Images Solutions
33b	Dennis Avon/Ardea.com	79	Nigel Dennis/NHPA	163	Anipix/Panorama Publishers
34b	Dennis Avon/Ardea.com	82a	Digital Images Solutions	164	Dennis Avon/Ardea.com
35	Lynn M. Stone/naturepl.com/	84	Stephen Dalton/NHPA	166	Digital Images Solutions
	Photo Access	88	Michael Durham/naturepl.com/	171	www.imagesofafrica.co.za
36	Kenneth Fink/Ardea.com		Photo Access	172	Digital Images Solutions
37a	Daniel Zupanc/NHPA	92	www.imagesofafrica.co.za	174	www.imagesofafrica.co.za
37b	James Warwick/NHPA	93	Digital Images Solutions	176b	Digital Images Solutions
38	www.imagesofafrica.co.za	95	Mary Clay/Ardea.com	179	Anipix/Panorama Publishers
41	Photo Access	100	Ulrike Schanze/naturepl.com/	180	JanekSzymanowski/
42b	Donald Trounson/Ardea.com		Photo Access		www.imagesofafrica.co.za
43a	Jean-Michel Labat/Ardea.com	101	Nigel Dennis/NHPA	180–182	www.imagesofafrica.co.za